CROSSING THE FLOOR

Humphry Berkeley

CROSSING THE FLOOR

London · George Allen & Unwin Ltd
Ruskin House Museum Street

First published in 1972

ISBN 0 04 329015 9

Printed in Great Britain
in 11 point Baskerville type by
Unwin Brothers Limited Woking and London

FOR JAMES SKINNER
my close friend and business partner
and his family
in the solitude of whose home
I wrote this book

Acknowledgments

I am grateful to Sir Alec Douglas-Home for making available to me the considerable correspondence which passed between us on the subject of electing a future Leader of the Conservative Party. I am also grateful to Mr Harold Wilson for allowing me to reproduce a letter which he wrote to me from 10 Downing Street.

The Rt Hon. Richard Wood, MP and Mr Tam Dalyell, MP have kindly allowed me to reproduce personal letters from them relating to The Sexual Offences Bill, 1966.

I am indebted to Mr George Gale, the Editor of the *Spectator*, for allowing me to incorporate in the chapter on the United Nations the greater part of an article which was published in the *Spectator*.

My grateful thanks are also due to James Skinner who has read the entire manuscript of this book and given me excellent advice, and to my sister Jane Russell and my secretary Shila Ladak who typed the manuscript.

I must state with regret, although not with surprise, that the Prime Minister, Mr Edward Heath, has refused permission for me to publish a handwritten letter which he sent to me expressing his thanks for the part which I played in the securing of his election as Party Leader in 1965. This letter remains in my possession.

July 1971

Contents

Illustrations

Introduction

In July 1970 I applied to join the Labour Party. To change one's party has a certain therapeutic effect and even unexpectedly beneficial consequences. I have found that all my real friends have been charming; I have made a complete new range of acquaintances. Those who cut me dead, and they are numerous, are people whom I never cared for anyway. I suppose that to such people the contents of this book will be regarded as rather worse than most current pornography but, by a slender margin, stopping short of profanity.

Some people, among whom I must include some members of my family, are ashamed, on my behalf, of what I have done. To them it seems slightly discreditable that in my middle forties, after a public school education, Cambridge, seven years as a Conservative MP and a reasonably successful business career I should take a step which they would have looked upon with indulgence had I taken it twenty years ago. Then, so they argue, I would of course have become older and wiser.

Other people prefer to regard what I have done as being a joke; they cannot take it seriously. Their attitude can be summed up in a conversation that I had recently with the mother-in-law of one of my friends, an agreeable, apparently intelligent, elderly, but not unworldly woman. We were chatting after dinner about this and when she said, 'Humphry, I know that you have joined the Labour Party but you surely don't want to see a Labour Government returned to power', I was astonished and asked her why she supposed that I was a subscribing member of the Westminster Constituency Labour Party unless I had that precise purpose in mind. A verbal chasm opened between us. She murmured something to the effect that she had supposed that I was only making a political gesture. I felt as though I was struggling with cotton wool. After she had sat in stunned silence for several minutes her son-in-law took her home.

The purpose of this book is to explain as coherently as I can what led me to join the Labour Party. I am not trying to gloss over anything, still less am I trying to justify myself in order to be rid of a guilt complex, or to build a political myth. I recognize that I attracted ridicule when I rejoined the Conservative Party in September 1969 only to leave it again a few months later. But how many political figures can totally escape ridicule without rewriting history or at some time suppressing their views? I have tried to avoid these remedies.

I feel no guilt towards the members of my family, who throughout the centuries have possessed a power of survival which few other families in this country can rival. They can look after themselves.

At the age of nine, after the death of my father, I was summoned to see my paternal great-aunt. 'I want you always to remember, Humphry', she said, 'that no Berkeley has ever been afraid of any living being. I want you to live up to that.' This was a daunting challenge to a boy of nine but I have tried to meet it throughout my life.

I do, from time to time, feel a sense of unease when I remember the rank-and-file members of the Lancaster Conservative Association. I have countless recollections of canvassing housing estates and blocks of flats with seemingly tireless middle-aged women, and of having cups of tea in their homes. I remember at election times touring committee rooms and seeing these same women after midnight, their faces grey with fatigue, addressing envelopes and filling them. An intense personal affection grew up between myself and my Conservative supporters in Lancaster, at least on my side. Almost all of them were in tears at midnight on 31 March 1966 when the count was over in the Lancaster Town Hall and my defeat was known. In particular, I remember my agent Leslie Bottell, a man of great efficiency, of extraordinary industry, and of total personal loyalty. I am the only person who knows that he personally disagreed with almost everything that I said, because, although we spoke quite freely to each other, he never hinted to anybody that he and his Member were other than completely united—as indeed we were in mutual trust.

I do not hear from Lancaster now, and I sometimes wonder if

my former supporters and Leslie Bottell feel hurt and let down by what I have done. If they feel that I have not been true to them by joining the Labour Party, I hope that they will try to understand that I would not have been true to myself had I done anything else.

Since my departure, the Conservative Party has moved further in the direction I most feared. In Rhodesia as a result of the settlement reached by Sir Alec Douglas-Home and Mr Ian Smith on 24th November 1971, evil has won. I pledge my moral and material support to the true representatives of the five million Africans of Rhodesia who are now at the mercy of a fiercely racialistic European minority which constitutes less than five per cent of the people of the country. My departure from the Conservative Party has been fully vindicated, but my heart is sick.

Chapter 1

My Political Background

I sat in the House of Commons as Conservative Member for Lancaster from October 1959 until March 1966. I won two elections but, although my first Parliament lasted for a full five years, my second term lasted only eighteen months, until Parliament was abruptly dissolved by the reigning Prime Minister. I cannot pretend that I was particularly uncomfortable in the Conservative Party even though I was commonly thought to be on the extreme left wing of the Party. I was also regarded as a rebel although I can only recall having voted against the Party whip or having abstained about half a dozen times, apart from the occasion of the Commonwealth Immigrants Bill of 1962 when I abstained throughout. My rebellions were not invariably understood. When I voted against the Government in favour of the renunciation of peerages, the *Lancaster Guardian* carried the headline 'Berkeley defies Whip'. I recall a man coming up to me after a meeting in Lancaster and saying in a salacious whisper, 'I did not like to ask you in public, but would you mind telling me what you said when you defied your Whip?' I had distinctly more trouble from my constituents than I did from the Conservative Whips. The former, on the whole, disapproved of my views on African advance. They also disapproved of my support for the abolition of capital punishment and of my introduction in February 1966 of a measure – which is now law – to make homosexual acts committed in private between consenting male adults no longer a crime.

I have frequently been described as a political maverick. While it is difficult for a person with strongly held views – which he does not hesitate to express – to have a record of complete consistency, I can fairly claim to have been as consistent as any other figure in contemporary politics. In 1961 I abstained on the second reading of the Southern Rhodesia Bill because I believed that its constitutional provisions were bad. In 1962 the Rhodesian Front was elected to power under this constitution, and thereafter UDI was inevitable. In July 1963 I spoke in the House of Commons in favour of a complete embargo on the sale of arms to South Africa. This was a year before a resolution to this effect was passed by the Security Council of the United Nations. I delivered my maiden speech on the controversial subject of advocating the release of Dr Banda from jail; a year later I became the first Conservative to make the same plea on behalf of Jomo Kenyatta. I have never regretted making these proposals, which I believe history has proved to be right.

In 1961 I voted and spoke against the Government in favouring the renunciation of peerages; but I was not to foresee that the principal beneficiary of this progressive measure would be Sir Alec Douglas-Home. Before the retirement of Macmillan was even suggested in public I advocated, in the spring of 1963, that in future the Conservative Party Leader should be chosen by a secret ballot of Conservative Members of Parliament. This became the practice in 1965.

When I entered Parliament in 1959, I had already been Chairman of the Cambridge University Conservative Association, President of the Union, and Chairman of the Coningsby Club (a dining club of Conservatives from Oxford and Cambridge). I was the secretary of the Carlton Club political committee. I had been the Conservative Parliamentary Candidate for Southall when I was only twenty-five, in 1951. Also, I had been for several years a senior official of the Conservative Political Centre. So I could hardly have had more impeccable credentials. I entered the House in the belief that there lay in front of me a conventional and reasonably successful political career.

At that time I did not regard myself as being particularly on the left wing of the Party; indeed, three years earlier I had actually supported the Suez adventure, and did not realize its utter futility – whether militarily successful or not – until some years later. My father, Reginald Berkeley, it is true, had been a Liberal Member of Parliament, but as he had died when I was aged nine he had not had a profound influence on the development of my political thinking. I had always been in favour of the abolition of capital punishment. The publication of the Wolfenden Report in 1957 convinced me that the law relating to homosexuality needed revision along the lines proposed by the Report. I regarded myself as a man of the centre in the tradition of R. A. Butler, Iain Macleod and Sir Edward Boyle.

In 1958 something happened which, though I did not recognize it at the time, came ultimately to turn me into the Socialist which I am today. In that year I visited Africa, going first to the Federation of Rhodesia and Nyasaland and later to Ghana. I was as exhilarated by Ghana as I was appalled by the Federation. Previously, I had never given much thought to African affairs: before I went to Africa I assumed that Africans were by definition primitive and would need a long period of tutelage before they could be granted independence. I did not meet any African politicians in Rhodesia in 1958, but was disconcerted to find that Africans were not allowed into European hotels, and that in Salisbury they had to use separate entrances in banks and post offices and other public buildings. I was affronted at the way in which recent immigrants from Britain to Rhodesia spoke disparagingly about Africans in front of their own African servants. This was not the partnership between the races which I had been told that Federation would bring about; on the contrary I saw a gross and growing inequality between the Africans and the Europeans.

By contrast, Nkrumah's independent Ghana was exactly twelve months old. A flourishing Westminster-type democracy seemed to exist. The ministers and, more particularly, the senior civil servants were clearly men of considerable ability, many of whom would have got to the top in any Western society. There was no colour discrimination or any apparent self-consciousness about colour, or prejudice against the white man. At the time I did not realize how frail a plant Westminster democracy was in an African state, nor did I realize that a Westminster-type constitution could, without additional safeguards, be turned quite legally into a tyranny, as was to happen in Nkrumah's last years. I believed then – and the return to constitutional government in Ghana under Dr Busia has confirmed my belief – that the Ghanaian is an extrovert lover of freedom, gay and uninhibited, and very easy for an Englishman to understand. The parliamentary debates held in the summer of 1959, before my entry to Parliament in October of that year, on the Hola incident and on the emergency in Nyasaland made me determined to specialize in African affairs when I reached Westminster. The Devlin Report merely reinforced my belief that all was far from well in the Federation of Rhodesia and Nyasaland, and the speech on Hola made by Enoch Powell was the most impressive statement that I had ever read on the duties of those who govern in relation to the governed.

This book is not intended to be anything as portentous as an autobiography: I have ahead of me, I hope, many years of active political life. Nevertheless I reached a milestone in my life in July 1970 when I applied to join the Labour Party—after having been an active Conservative politician for more than twenty years. I have tried here to set down the development of my political thinking which led to my taking a step which would have astonished me had it been prophesied ten years earlier. I have also attempted to portray some of the leading politicians who influenced my political development. Inevitably these portraits are subjective and at times they may bear the marks of the hothouse atmosphere of Westminster. In Britain however back-bench MPs have a much closer view of our rulers than happens in most countries because ministers are also Members of Parliament. While the House of Commons has ceased for many years to be the best club in Europe (if it ever was) Members of Parliament, whether ministers or not, are thrown into each other's company and into physical proximity—if only because the Chamber of the House of Commons is so small, and the dining and recreational facilities are so inadequate. Many people will find my judgment of Mr Heath somewhat harsh. He has, however, destroyed at least for the time being that part of the Conservative Party to which I belonged—namely the liberal wing. Not surprisingly I regarded this wing as the most valuable asset of the Conservative Party. Its revival is necessary if the Conservative Party is to remain a party of government. All those who believe, as I do, in the soundness of the two-party system must hope that one day it will be reborn.

In particular I have written about those matters about which I care most: immigration, race relations, Africa, the Commonwealth, and the United Nations. It is in relation to these issues that I should be judged.

Chapter 2

The Conservative Party

The Conservative Party is an extraordinary institution. Even though I have belonged to it for twenty-one years, it remains for me to some extent an enigma. Its most compelling motive is a desire for power. Its members regard a period of opposition with incredulity, as a brief interlude which must be brought to an end at the earliest opportunity. In this century no Conservative Leader has survived three electoral defeats in a row; nor is it conceivable that he would be allowed to do so. One defeat is not easily forgiven, as Sir Alec Douglas-Home discovered in 1965. Had Churchill not been a national figure transcending party loyalties, it is doubtful if he would have survived his second narrow defeat in 1950. Baldwin was nearly butchered in 1930; and people were already discussing how Edward Heath could most speedily be disposed of during the 1970 election campaign when a Labour victory seemed certain.

A large number of Labour MPs are happier when their party is in opposition—they regard their party as one of protest rather than one of power. Some of them would rather lie down in Trafalgar Square than man Government Departments. I have never met a Conservative who relished opposition. For the most part they find it bewildering and uncomfortable, and for this reason the Conservative Party is not seen at its best when out of power.

For a party which professes a regard for personal freedom the Conservative Party is strangely authoritarian. Its policy is laid down by its Leader who himself, until recently, was not elected but emerged through a system which nobody could explain. There were no rules, and such conventions as existed could quite ruthlessly be broken by the king-makers, who in recent years always included the Chief Whip and the Chairman of the 1922 Committee, and frequently the Chairman of the Party.

In three cases in the present century the Conservative Party has actually had an heir-apparent who became Prime Minister and Party Leader without any discussion or consultation at all. Ironically, each of them – Balfour, Neville Chamberlain and Eden – was to see his premiership end in disaster.

Not only does the Conservative Party Leader determine Party policy, he also chooses, in the rare instance of opposition, the members of his Shadow Cabinet, and he appoints the Chief Whip and the Chairman and Vice-Chairmen of the Conservative Central Office which is his personal machine.

A Conservative Party Leader may, as Mr Heath did, set up a number of advisory study groups to help him formulate future policy. But, as I know from having served on one, these groups are purely advisory, and are by no means confined to MPs. I have never known the Conservative Parliamentary Party debate policy with a view to establishing a majority position, let alone to take a vote. Nor have I ever witnessed anything approaching a dialogue on policy between the Party Leader and the back-benchers. I have frequently attended meetings of the 1922 Committee which were addressed by Mr Macmillan, Sir Alec Douglas-Home and Mr Heath when they were Party Leaders, but questions were only permitted afterwards, and these were usually only of a level that could be expected from a ward meeting in a constituency. Meetings are held from time to time between the Party Leader and the Executive Committee of the 1922 Committee or its Chairman, but as policy is so rarely discussed by the 1922 Committee as a whole it is difficult to see how this can be a genuine two-way movement of ideas.

I do not wish to suggest that policy is not discussed by Conservative MPs collectively, but such a discussion would usually take place in a Party committee. I have known some acrimonious discussions—notably over Africa, immigration, resale price maintenance and the European Community, but the choice of back-bench speakers is left to the Chairman of the Committee and it is left to the visiting minister or the Whip in attendence to interpret the spirit of the meeting to the party leadership. The Conservative Party dislikes intensely an appearance of disunity; its differences take place behind closed doors. No voting occurs, no press briefings are given, although not infrequently press leakages do occur. From time to time *ad hoc* groups are formed, usually when the Conservatives are in power, with the aim of opposing Government policy. The group led by Churchill to oppose the India Act, and that led by Sir Derek Walker-Smith and Mr Neil Marten to oppose Britain's entry into the Common Market, are cases in point. Such groups are rare and are unpopular with the leaders, the Whips and the rank-and-file.

The whole organization of the Conservative Party in Parliament is based upon the assumption that a Conservative Government will be in power. Mr Heath was the first Leader of the Conservative Party for over forty years who had not already become Prime Minister before he was formally elected Leader. Bonar Law was thought to be somewhat pedantic in requiring the Party meeting to elect him Leader – even though he was not opposed – immediately before he became Prime Minister in October 1922. It has been suggested that if a vacancy in the premiership were to occur during a period when it was the governing party, it would in some way interfere with the royal prerogative if the Conservative Party were in future to elect a Leader in advance of the official appointment and kissing of hands. This, however, is merely to say that the Queen should be expected to do for the Conservative Party what it ought to be able to do for itself.

The fact that the Party Leader in opposition appoints his own deputy, chooses the members of the Shadow Cabinet and allocates them 'shadow' portfolios suggests that in the eyes of the Conservative Party opposition is exceptional rather than normal. While a Labour Prime Minister in practice has as much power as a Conservative Prime Minister, the constitution of the Labour Party suggest that opposition rather than government is considered its normal state. In opposition, the Labour Shadow Cabinet is elected by the Parliamentary Party, as is the Deputy Leader and the Chief Whip. The Leader is elected annually and can be challenged—as in fact Gaitskell was challenged on one occasion by Harold Wilson. There is no doubt that the Labour Party, if in power, would insist upon electing a Leader if there was to be a vacancy before the Queen could appoint a new Prime Minister.

At first sight a Labour back-bench MP appears to be bound by a series of Party rules which are not applied to his Conservative equivalent. First, he has to agree to obey a forbidding list of standing orders which permit an abstention only on a matter of conscience and explicitly forbid a vote against a party whip.* Secondly, he is bound by decisions on policy made by the Parliamentary Labour Party—though, unlike his Conservative counterpart, he will have recorded his vote on the matter in question at a full meeting of the Parliamentary Labour Party. Thirdly, he is not permitted the luxury of attacking his colleagues in public; and fourthly, he is not permitted to table an early day motion without the consent of the Chief Whip.

In practice, however, a Conservative MP is the more likely to be muzzled. In the Conservative Party there is an unwritten code of conduct which owes something in its origins to Dr Arnold, the barrack square, and Dr Squeers of Dotheboys Hall. Instead of the formal Party meeting at which the offending Labour member is denied the whip by a majority vote, the erring Conservative has to face prep-school bullying, social ostracism, and in more serious cases an undermining of his position in his own constituency.

Aneurin Bevan, Stafford Cripps, Sidney Silverman and Michael Foot have all gaily had the whip withdrawn from them only to have it restored in good time for the next election. Anthony Nutting, Nigel Nicolson and Sir Frank Medlicott are grisly casualties of the consequences of opposing their party over Suez. In 1961, after opposing the Government on the issue of the renunciation of peerages, I discovered that my own Whip, who lived in my constituency, was gently but firmly suggesting to the officers of my constituency Conservative Association that they should look for another candidate for the next election.

*The Labour vote on 28 October 1971 when 69 Labour MPs voted against a three-line whip suggests that there is safety in numbers.

The nature of Conservative MPs has undergone a change for the worse during the last twenty years. There have always been a proportion of Conservative MPs who were vulgar, exhibitionst, self-centred, self-interested, self-seeking and even, on rare occasions, actually delinquent. There is, however, a type of MP who has been unique to the Conservative Party of which perhaps Sir Harry Legge-Bourke is a good contemporary example. He is a gentle honourable man, incapable, I would judge, of telling an untruth, totally without personal ambition, who sees his membership of Parliament as an act of public service. He belongs unhappily to a dying breed. He and those like him are being replaced by human efficiency machines, constructed for utility rather than grace. They reel off figures to anybody who is prepared to listen—these statistics not infrequently include the size of their own parliamentary majorities. They have not learned the art of conversation. They appear to communicate by conducting a series of interviews with each other. This breed exists, of course, on both sides of the House although I sense that at present it predominates in the Conservative Party. For them the House of Commons is the stepping-stone to the glittering prizes of office and power. They have contributed towards the lowering of the esteem in which Parliament is held by the public.

I was always an object of suspicion among some Conservative MPs, particularly among those vicious, uncouth bullies who habitually clustered around the centre table in the House of Commons smoking room. These were the people who spread it about that I was in favour of black rule in Africa because it was to my commercial advantage to press for this. In fact the reverse was true. I was asked to resign from the Board of John Howard & Company (Africa) Limited, and did so, after I had entertained Kenneth Kaunda in London before the dissolution of the Federation of Rhodesia and Nyasaland. My co-directors felt, and they were right, that Sir Roy Welensky would not have approved of such behaviour. I did not rejoin the Board until after the independence of Zambia. Some of Lord Salisbury's family took the myth of my business interests even further. A friend of mine was told when staying at Hatfield that I owned the greater part of Zambia's copper. I wish that this had been true. I have never in fact possessed a single copper share.

The widespread nature of these entirely false rumours can perhaps best be illustrated by an account of a conversation between two senior Conservative back-benchers in the smoking room which was overheard by one of my friends in 1964.

'Did you see that disgraceful photograph of Humphry Berkeley presenting a petition about South African political prisoners to South Africa House?'

'Yes, and I hear that he marched to Trafalgar Square arm in arm with Barbara Castle.'

'You know that he drives a Rolls-Royce?'

'That means nothing; here today and gone tomorrow.'

'Why is he so interested in Black Africa?'

'He runs some bank, I believe, called the Bank of Ethiopia.'*

'What is its credit rating?' 'Shaky.'

It is a characteristic of the Conservative Party that those who run it like to do so with the minimum of rules—or preferably with no rules at all. In this way the school captain can act as umpire as well. In the spring of 1963, when I suggested in a speech to the Chelsea Young Conservatives – a speech which attracted some publicity – that in future a Conservative Leader should be elected by the secret ballot of all Conservative MPs, this proposal was treated with ridicule. I made the suggestion deliberately and timed it for that moment since I already had a feeling that Macmillan wished to deny the succession to Butler. Lord Aldington, then Deputy Chairman of the Conservative Party and a devoted friend of Butler, challenged me at the Carlton Club: 'Humphry, surely you are not advocating one man, one vote?' He was as incredulous as if I had suggested that the Leader of the Conservative Party should be elected by the entire adult population of the African continent. He was scarcely mollified when I replied that all parliamentary legislation rested upon the fact that the vote of one MP was equal to that of another. He took the view that openly-competing candidates for the leadership would imply a deep Party split.

In October 1963 Macmillan's resignation was announced

*As far as I know, no 'Bank of Ethiopia' exists!

to the Conservative Party Conference. I believe that I was the first person to inform Lord Hailsham of the resignation, when I did so at the entrance of the Imperial Hotel, Blackpool. He seemed flabbergasted and talked of calling a press conference. Although he was not my choice for Leader I admired him as a friend and I told him that if I were in his position I would announce at the CPC meeting that he was due to address that evening that he intended to renounce his peerage—which in fact he did. For good measure I told him, since there were no rules, what I would also do in his position, namely get one of his supporters to demand that the Party Leader should be elected by the Conference itself, then in session. I believe that this demand would have been impossible for the Chairman of the Conference, Dame Margaret Shepherd, to resist. Quintin demurred at this advice, saying 'I shall only make myself very unpopular'. In fact he made himself very unpopular with his colleagues anyway because, wherever he went, he was greeted with frenzied enthusiasm which he did nothing to discourage. As I predicted to him, once the Conference was over his cause was lost.

After the Conference ended and before Lord Home became Prime Minister I wrote the following letter to *The Times*.

15 October, 1963

Sir,

The customary method of choosing a Conservative Party Leader has on this occasion broken down before the process has started.

The essence of the system was secrecy of consultation, the absence of openly-competing candidates, and, where there was no heir-apparent, such speed of action that the matter was settled and over before the rank-and-file of the Party was aware what had happened.

The announcement of the Prime Minister's impending resignation to the Conservative Party Conference, the absence of any formalized procedure, the uncertainty as to who is entitled to be consulted and the lack of a properly constituted electoral college has created a situation of unprecedented confusion.

Each of the 5,000 delegates at Blackpool has assumed the right, if not to be consulted, at least to demonstrate his choice publicly by applause, rapturous or muted, or even by silence. Where is this to end? Before long we may have a poll of all paid-up members of the Conservative Party, or even a referendum of all those who voted Conservative at the last election. We would then have adopted the American system of primaries and party conventions.

It was because I felt that the traditional way of choosing a Conservative Leader was utterly inadequate that I suggested last March, before the leadership was in dispute, that the Party should agree upon a more suitable and less irregular system in which a small electoral college, in which Members of Parliament predominated, should elect a Leader by secret ballot. Had this been done, the fever at Blackpool would have been unnecessary and irrelevant.

Obviously it would be impossible to devise rules now to deal with a situation which is already upon us. But the clear lesson of the past week is that the old method can never be used again and that we must agree upon a procedure which avoids both secret manipulation and mass participation.

Yours faithfully,

HUMPHRY BERKELEY

I then took up with the new Prime Minister, Sir Alec Douglas-Home, the need to have clear, definite and obviously democratic rules for the election of a future Leader.

I wrote to Sir Alec as follows on 1 January 1964.

Dear Prime Minister,

In March of last year, before the leadership of the Party was in dispute, I said in public that I felt that the Conservative Party should adopt a more formal method of choosing a Leader. The events of the Blackpool Conference and after have, in my view, emphasized this need and would have done so, whoever had emerged as Leader of the Party.

Since then, I have had many talks with our colleagues in the House, including senior members of the Government. I have discovered a widespread view that we should not continue with the present system which, in any event, as practised a few months ago, bore little resemblance to what has been known as the customary process.

The fact that the Chief Whip felt obliged to reveal in public a part but not all of the results of his soundings is evidence of the misgivings which are felt about the present process throughout the Party.

No doubt there are different views as to what formalized system should be adopted. Some would advocate a secret ballot of Members of Parliament voting for openly competing candidates. Others might extend the electoral college by including representatives of the candidates, the National Union and Peers in receipt of the Party Whip. All these possibilities might be explored.

Would you consider, as Leader of the Party, setting up a small Committee to consider this matter, hear opinions and make recommendations? I am sure that the whole issue could be considered more calmly at a time when there is no likelihood of its having to be implemented for some considerable period.

Nothing which I have said, of course, implies any criticism of your Leadership of the Party.

May I take this opportunity of sending you every good wish for an outstandingly successful year.

Yours,

HUMPHRY BERKELEY

Sir Alec replied on 14 January, 'I am not averse to the idea of a private study of the methods which might be used on some future occasion, but I do not think that it would be wise to initiate this before the election. It would inevitably become known, and would then be taken as evidence of dissatisfaction with the present leadership—although I appreciate your assurance that it does not.' Sir Alec invited me to be in touch with him later in the year.

I replied to the Prime Minister on 21 January 1964 that I and my friends were 'all happy to leave the matter in abeyance until after the election', although I went on to say that the prospective study 'should not be so private as to prevent all interested parties from giving their views quite freely'.

After the 1964 General Election when the Conservatives went into opposition, Sir Alec Douglas-Home, on 5 November 1964, informed a meeting of the 1922 Committee that he proposed to hold a review of the mechanism for choosing the Leader of the Party. I immediately wrote to Sir Alec and subsequently saw him and formulated my own ideas on how the Party Leader should be elected.

On 3 December 1964 I took part in a televised debate at the Oxford Union. I solemnly read out a letter purporting to be from Breshnev to Khrushchev, who had recently been deposed, which I claimed had come into my possession. The letter, which brought the house down, read:

> *My dear Nikita,*
>
> I have known for some time of your wish to return to private life. Some months ago you told me that you desired to give way to a younger man. I feel that the time has come when we can no longer impose on your sense of duty and self-sacrifice.
>
> I know that you will not be able to get about as much in the future as you have in the past. Indeed, I am advised that you may not be able to leave your house again.
>
> I am sure that you will be glad to know that we have set in motion the customary processes of consultation from which your successor will emerge.
>
> *Yours sincerely. . .*

When I next saw the Soviet Ambassador at a party in his Embassy, he affected to be amused. He seemed to be less pleased when I said, 'At least we are trying to get our system changed'.

Appendix I of this book contains the (previously unpublished) complete correspondence between Sir Alec Douglas-Home and myself. It is clear from this correspondence that my initiative and subsequent meetings with Sir Alec resulted in the new system which Sir Alec announced in February 1965, which was almost identical to the proposals which I had made in my memorandum of 9 December 1964.

My proposals and Sir Alec's final decision appear in Appendix II of this book. Sir Alec's decision and my proposals differ in only two repects. He proposed that the victorious candidate must have 15 per cent more votes cast than any other candidate. This did not happen in 1965 at the time of Mr Heath's election since – owing to his bare overall majority – his opponents withdrew. I also recommended that the Leader should periodically be re-elected. I believe this still to be desirable.

As is known, Mr Edward Heath became Leader of the Party in July 1965. Since Iain Macleod was not a candidate by his own choice, I voted for Mr Heath. Ironically, had I voted for Mr Maudling, as I now wish I had done, Mr Heath would not have achieved an overall majority over the other two candidates, and a second ballot might have been necessary. Although I now have great reservations about my choice, and the Conservative Party has even greater reservations about me, I am happy to have pioneered a reform which, at least, has brought the Conservative Party into the twentieth century and should spare it from ever again going through the agony of October 1963.

Chapter 3

Immigration and Race

I do not remember immigration being an issue between the parties before 1959. Sir Cyril Osborne, the Conservative MP for Louth, had attracted to himself some notoriety by advocating restrictions on the right of coloured Commonwealth citizens to settle in Britain. His views were unattractive to me and did not seem to command general support. In fact the number of coloured immigrants from the Commonwealth had grown rapidly during the late 1950s, and by 1961 the Government decided that it must take action.

The passing of the Commonwealth Immigrants Act in the year 1962 placed restrictions on the hitherto absolute right of Commonwealth citizens to enter Britain. I could not support this measure and throughout its stages in the House of Commons I abstained from voting. I remember Hugh Gaitskell making the greatest oration that I ever heard in the House of Commons against the Bill. I was moved by his oratory and I agreed with his arguments. In retrospect I have come to believe that I was wrong, and that it was necessary for the sake of harmonious race relations to limit the number of immigrants who did not hold United Kingdom passports entering this country.

There was, however, a special category of British subject for whom special provision was made in the early 1960s. As Tanganyika, Uganda and Kenya moved towards independence I recall many meetings of the Conservative Parliamentary Commonwealth Affairs Committee at which pledges were extracted from successive Colonial Secretaries, including Mr Duncan Sandys, to grant United Kingdom citizenship to Asians in East Africa. What ensued was no loop-hole in the law, as Mr Sandys subsequently alleged. On the contrary, fearing that they might suffer from the consequences of independence and African rule, the British Government deliberately offered United Kingdom citizenship – which involved an unrestricted right of entry into Britain – to all Asians in East Africa unless they were second-generation immigrants—that is to say unless they and in addition one of their parents had been born in East Africa. However, any Asian or European resident in Africa could apply for local nationality within two years of the granting of independence. Most Asians who had a choice opted for United Kingdom citizenship in the belief that a United Kingdom passport carried with it the right to enter the United Kingdom.

In 1965 the first Labour Government introduced a Race Relations Bill, although I did not at that time appreciate the urgency for legislative action. By 1964, however, it was clear that immigration had become a potentially explosive issue when Mr Patrick Gordon-Walker, Labour's first Foreign Secretary, was beaten at the General Election in the safe Labour seat of Smethwick by Mr Peter Griffiths in a campaign which had centred on immigration. I sent Mr Gordon-Walker a telegram expressing my sympathy. Despite the fact that I fought the 1966 General Election as a Conservative candidate, I was glad that Mr Griffiths was then beaten by Mr Andrew Faulds and that Smethwick reverted to being a Labour seat. In my view Mr Heath, who was by then the Leader of the Conservative Party, should have refused to endorse the candidature of Mr Griffiths.

In 1967, Mr Duncan Sandys and Mr Enoch Powell made a series of speeches in which they drew attention to what they described as the loop-hole in the law which allowed United Kingdom passport holders of Asian origin to enter this country. They called for the law to be changed. As a result, anticipating that the law might be changed, growing numbers of East African Asians arrived in Britain. In what I regarded as a wholly unnecessary mood of alarm the Labour Home Secretary, assisted by his Parliamentary Under-Secretary, Mr David Ennals, introduced into Parliament the 1968 Commonwealth Immigrants Act which for the first time had the effect of making United Kingdom passport holders stateless persons, since it denied the right of entry into Britain to those who were of Asian descent. This was, in my judgment, a shameful measure which involved the British Government in a breach of faith. As Iain Macleod wrote in the *Spectator* of 23 February 1968 referring to the pledges given to the Asians in East Africa: 'I gave my word. I meant to give it. I wish to keep it.' I hope that a future Labour Government will repeal this measure.

In April 1968 the Labour Government introduced a new Race Relations Bill which the Conservative Party decided to oppose. The evidence of the Street Report committee, of which Sir Geoffrey Howe, the present Conservative Solicitor-General, was a member, and that of the PEP Report clearly showed that racial discrimination in the United Kingdom was increasing, particularly with regard to housing and employment, and could only be abated by further legislation. I then decided that I could no longer remain a member of the Conservative Party and I wrote the following letter to Mr Heath.

17 April, 1968

Dear Ted,

I write to tell you, with very great regret, that the time has come when I must leave the Conservative Party.

I was shocked to read of the decision of the Shadow Cabinet to oppose the Race Relations Bill by means of a reasoned amendment, particularly since I had been assured by a member of the Shadow Cabinet only a few weeks ago that the Opposition intended to support the measure in principle. I agree that the Bill as it stands is not in every respect satisfactory, but the reasoned amendment seems to me to be of a wholly negative character.

I feel personally involved in this issue since, as Honorary Treasurer of the United Kingdom Committee for Human Rights Year, in company with my fellow officers I signed the statement on April 10 warmly welcoming the Race Relations Bill as a step in the right direction.

As I think you know, I have also been unhappy for some time over the trend of Conservative policy in relation to Rhodesia. I do not believe that an honourable settlement consistent with the six principles can be negotiated with the

Smith regime. It seemed to me, both at the Conservative Party Conference and also in the debate in Parliament at the end of last month, that the Conservative Party takes a different view.

I hope that the British Government will support the strengthening of sanctions at the United Nations and it is clear that the Conservative Party would resist such measures.

I was also profoundly unhappy at your statement before Christmas that the Conservative Party would resume the sale of arms to South Africa which could not be used to enforce the policies of apartheid. I do not believe that such a distinction is valid.

I had hoped that my differences with the Conservative Party could have been confined to the issues of Southern Africa, important though these are. I now find myself in apparent disagreement with the Party on a much broader front.

It is my fear that on the whole issue of race, which is to some extent inter-related to the problems of Southern Africa, the Conservative Party is committing itself to an attitude which I believe to be wrong. I think therefore that my only honest course of action is to resign from membership of the Party.

I take this step with very great regret since 20 years ago I was Chairman of the Cambridge University Conservative Association, I have served for 8 years as a member of the staff of the Conservative Central Office and have sat in the House of Commons for 6½ years as a Conservative Member of Parliament.

I would like, if you have no objection, to release this letter to the Press.

Yours ever,
HUMPHRY
(*Humphry Berkeley*)

3 *Lowndes Street S.W.*1.

On 18 April 1968 Mr Heath replied at considerable length:

Dear Humphry,

I was sorry to receive your letter of April 17, 1968, telling me of your intention of resigning from the Conservative Party because of its policies on the Race Relations Bill, Rhodesia and the sale of arms for external defence to South Africa.

There is no difference of objective between you and the Party in opposing racial and religious discrimination. At the start of the last General Election campaign I stated publicly that such discrimination would not be tolerated in the Party. This remains the Party's position.

But in matters as complex and difficult as race relations it is understandable that there should be differing and deeply-held views as to how this purpose can best be achieved. Our front-bench speakers will deploy the arguments in the debate on the Second Reading of the Race Relations Bill next Tuesday.

But I must deal now with the three points you raise in your letter.

First, there is no truth in your suggestion that the Shadow Cabinet changed its position on the Race Relations Bill. There was no prior consultation between the Government and the Opposition on the Bill, and the Shadow Cabinet first considered its contents and the attitude to be adopted towards it on Wednesday evening of last week, April 10, the day after the publication of the Bill.

The Shadow Cabinet was then in a position to take account of the views expressed by Conservative back-benchers at a well-attended meeting of the Parliamentary Party's Home Affairs Committee—a procedure which I understand you favour, and wish to see encouraged.

The Shadow Cabinet at its meeting decided to table a reasoned amendment. In so doing it was pursuing precisely the same course as it followed on the Race Relations Bill of 1965 – when you were yourself a Conservative MP – as a result of which considerable changes were later made in the Bill. I fail therefore to understand the sense of shock which you protest at the parliamentary action that the Shadow Cabinet decided to take.

Secondly, the policy announced last December on the sale of arms for external defence to South Africa is the same as that followed by the last Conservative Government. The distinction between different types of arms was maintained in practice then and can be so ordered again.

United Nations resolutions concerning arms to South Africa are not binding on any member. Moreover so far as arms for external defence are concerned the British Delegate to the United Nations specifically dissociated the Conservative Government from such resolutions on both occasions when they were passed. All this occurred, of course, while you remained a Conservative MP.

We see no justification for pursuing a policy denying the sale of such arms to South Africa which does nothing to help the Africans, but which weakens our South Atlantic defence, harms our international relations and severely damages our economy. Meantime, other countries take this opportunity from us and yet maintain harmonious relations with other African States.

Thirdly, the policy of the Conservative Party towards Rhodesia since UDI has been throughout, as you will again recall from your own time in the House, that a settlement must be obtained through negotiation for which sanctions were a means to an end.

If you reject this, you must face the alternative of either attempting to wage war on Rhodesia, thus causing chaos and intensifying racial hatred, or of abandoning any attempt to secure a multiracial society there in the future. For it is clear that sanctions of themselves cannot break the Rhodesian economy, nor are they bringing down the regime.

Whereas the maintenance of existing sanctions may contribute towards an eventual negotiation, to add more mandatory sanctions at this stage will only consolidate Rhodesian opinion more effectively behind UDI. For this reason, we shall oppose them in Parliament and shall concentrate on the attempt to secure an honourable negotiated settlement.

We do not disagree about the importance of racial problems throughout the world, not only between white and coloured peoples but just as much, and often more bitterly felt, between different coloured races themselves.

The Conservative Government maintained open immigration into Britain from the Commonwealth for as long as possible because of its commitment to the Commonwealth ideal. But no one can deny the problems that have since arisen from this attitude.

For my part, I am determined to do everything possible to prevent those tensions already existing in some of the big cities in our land from developing into the racial clashes which we see elsewhere.

But this cannot be done by the easy acceptance of legislation, much of it unworkable and parts of which tend to remove disadvantages only to create privileges, thereby intensifying personal resentments and endangering still further the effective solution of racial problems.

The situation can only be remedied by positive action, both corporate and personal, to improve human relations between the races, combined with the energetic pursuit of Government policies to provide the necessary housing, schools, and health services in the areas most affected. These must be based on a thriving economy which also offers the opportunities for employment required.

I am sorry that you no longer find yourself able to contribute to such policies in the Conservative Party for they are an essential element in alleviating the human misery and suffering which is the inevitable product of racial disharmony.

Yours sincerely,
TED HEATH

House of Commons

I regarded Mr Heath's arguments as terribly thin. At least the 1965 Bill was considerably amended. The reasoned amendment put forward by the Conservative Party then, for which I voted, raised a very substantial issue, the substance of which was that conciliation and fair employment practices, rather than criminal sanctions, were more appropriate to the field of race relations. The Labour Government took full account of the Conservative view and the final legislation reflected this fact. In 1968 the reasoned amendment was merely a device which enabled Mr Heath to say that the Conservative Party had not actually voted against the bill on its second reading.

I know how you feel Ted—ruddy left-wingers!

It was a vague statement implying that the Bill was simultaneously too weak and too strong. It offered no suggestions as to how the measure might be improved. As *The Times* first leading article of 19 April 1968 said by way of comment on my resignation from the Conservative Party, 'The reasoned amendment that the Shadow Cabinet have tabled is, however, a rejection of the Bill'.

I could not agree that the Shadow Cabinet had not changed its position for I knew that Sir Edward Boyle had voted for the East Africa Asian Bill on the express understanding that the Conservative Party would support the Race Relations Bill. He had told me so at dinner some weeks earlier. Before the mutually agreed release of our letters to the press, Mr Heath telephoned me and expressed his regret at my action. I told him that I thought that he was taking a thoroughly wrong stand in the mistaken view that he would preserve party unity. Mr Heath replied that if he had not opposed the Race Relations Bill in this way the Party would have split. I replied that it would split anyway, and so it proved to be.

At this moment Mr Enoch Powell chose to make his now notorious speech in Birmingham. Mr Powell has subsequently denied that it was inflammatory, yet, referring to the Race Relations Bill he said: 'To enact legislation at this moment is to risk throwing a match on to gunpowder.' He described this nation as 'busily engaged in heaping up its own funeral pyre'. Mr Heath was obliged to dismiss him from the Shadow Cabinet.

For me the most distressing trend in British public opinion has been the hardening of support in favour of even more restrictive measures against Commonwealth immigrants. As the speeches of Mr Powell grew wilder and more hysterical, so both parties almost seemed to outbid each other in a competition, the winner of which had to show that his policies would let fewer coloured people come into this country. By 1970 neither party was particularly courageous but Mr Heath, in order to appease his Powellite supporters, pledged that a Conservative Government would introduce immigration legislation which in one respect, namely the patrial clauses, actually went beyond what Powell himself was advocating, and drew his opposition on the Committee Stage of the Bill.

I have often wondered what motivated Mr Powell to make race and immigration the issues upon which his voice was heard loudest. The simplest explanation and the one most frequently given by orthodox members of the Conservative Party is that by 1968 Mr Powell had convinced himself that Mr Heath could not lead the party to victory and that he was making a direct bid to supplant him after the election. Certainly, Mr Powell's conduct during the 1970 General Election campaign strongly reinforces this supposition. It is, I believe, too simple an analysis.

While Mr Powell's views on race and immigration hit a particularly vulnerable point in the usually tolerant body of British public opinion, he has expressed views on other matters which were far from popular in his party or the country as a whole. He voted in favour of the abolition of hanging and for homosexual law reform. He publicly advocated the withdrawal of a British presence east of Suez. He even went so far as to declare that since England was a white man's country Rhodesia was a black man's country. He scoffed at the idea of further talks with Ian Smith and said that he did not believe that negotiations could produce a constitutional settlement for which he could vote in Parliament—though he simultaneously advocated the ending of sanctions since in his view they would never work.

Mr Powell's original speech on race in April 1968 did not come as a surprise to me. I had had, only a month earlier, a heated argument with Enoch's wife Pam at the wedding reception for Iain Macleod's daughter. She accused me and Nicholas Scott, Conservative MP for South Paddington, who was with me, of destroying the purity of the British race. She said that we knew nothing about the colour problem. She brushed aside the fact that Nicholas Scott had a large number of coloured immigrants in his constituency of South Paddington, on the grounds that he did not live among them as she and Enoch did in Wolverhampton. I had known Pam for twenty years. She was a secretary in my office before she married Enoch. I knew that she was devotedly loyal to her husband during his many ups and downs, and I knew that she would faithfully reflect his views.

I do not believe, as some people do, that Powell performed a public service in starting a national debate on a topic which had not been discussed before. In the first place it is not true: immigration and race were very fully discussed in 1962 and in 1965. At least one parliamentary constituency had been lost to Labour on the colour issue at a time when there was a national swing to Labour in the 1964 General Election.

I objected strongly to the content and language of Mr Powell's speeches which in some cases actually constituted, in my opinion, incitement to violence. I remembered the dockers demonstrating in Parliament Square and shouting to the High Commissioner for Kenya: 'Go back home, you dirty nigger.' I was ashamed that British people could behave in such a way and I feared that there might be repercussions overseas.

Unlike Mr Powell, I know many countries in Africa intimately, and I feared that the provocative nature of his speeches would not only generate a physical response in Britain but that they might lead to riots in Nairobi or Lusaka where a white minority lives at the top of the economic pyramid rather than its base as is the case with coloured people in Britain.

I have no doubt that Enoch Powell regards himself as a man of destiny. But men of destiny are dangerous people to have around unless their presence coincides with a moment of destiny in a nation's life to which they can respond. I have no doubt that Enoch Powell has been psychologically deeply affected by the loss of Empire, more perhaps than he recognizes. He served in the Indian Army and saw the evening splendour of the British Raj; like Winston Churchill before him he correctly diagnosed that if India went the Empire would collapse. Mr David Clarke, formerly Director of the Conservative Research Department, has described to me how Enoch came to see him in 1946 applying for a job, in the uniform of a Brigadier. He also told me that one of the first papers put up to the Shadow Cabinet by Enoch was a plan to hold India by force, a remedy which even Churchill was to reject. Had the Empire remained intact I do not believe that Enoch Powell would have objected to the presence in Britain, the heart of a magnificent edifice, of four or five million coloured subjects of the Crown. The loss of Empire was for Powell a spiritual amputation. If Britain no longer had possessions, the inhabitants of her former dependencies had no place in her national life. With ruthless logic this personally kind man seeks to rid Britain of any evidence of her imperial past, unaware of the suffering which he is causing to the coloured population and of the harm which he is doing to the British soul by inflaming dark passions and allowing them to smoulder.

I must with regret add that Mr Powell is sometimes distinctly slipshod in his use of facts relating to legislation on immigration and race relations. On 28 May 1971 he wrote an article in *The Times* which was entitled 'Guilty Silence on the Kenya Asians'. I wrote the following letter which stated the true position and which appeared in *The Times* on 31 May 1971:

Sir,

Mr Enoch Powell has become careless. It is incorrect to state, as he did in his article 'Guilty Silence on the Kenya Asians' that 'in fact under the new Kenyan law, the Asian inhabitants did not become Kenya citizens automatically on independence day but were allowed a subsequent option'.

The true facts are that any Asian who was born in Kenya, and one of whose parents was also born in Kenya, automatically became a Kenya citizen on independence day in 1963. Those Asians who did not fall within this category, that is to say first generation Kenya Asians, became entitled to United Kingdom and Colonies passports issued by the British High Commission unless they opted for Kenyan nationality within two years.

However, Mr Powell is incorrect on a much more important fact. The provisions made for Asians in Kenya were identical to those made for Asians in Uganda which became independent in 1962 and Tanganyika which became independent in 1961. It cannot, therefore, be true to say, as Mr Powell does, 'it therefore seemed to follow that this effect of the drafting of the 1962 (Commonwealth Immigrants) Act was unintentional and was only discovered subsequently to 1963. The alternative hypothesis of deliberate concealment appeared too discreditable to entertain'. There was nothing to conceal. The British High Commissioner in Tanganyika had already started to issue United Kingdom and Colonies passports to Asians in Tanganyika in 1961.

Not only is Mr Powell grossly inaccurate as to the legislative measures and their dates, but he is also inaccurate when he states that no assurances were given by the United Kingdom Government to anybody that Asian United Kingdom and Colonies citizens would be allowed automatic entry into this country from East Africa. I attended numerous meetings of the Conservative Parliamentary Commonwealth Affairs Committee between 1961 and 1963 and can confirm that assurances were sought and given by successive Colonial Secretaries that special provision would be made for East African Asians.

Having demolished Mr Powell's article so far, I wish I

could rescue him from the implications of what he said in his final paragraph. He wrote 'When the 1961 Bill was drafted and passed through Parliament nobody realized the consequences of the definition of "United Kingdom passport". By the end of 1963 these consequences had been spotted: but the Government of the day – or the ministers concerned – decided to stay mum and hope for the best.'

I have already pointed out that the situation was already known (and intended) when Tanganyika became independent in 1961. Why does Mr Powell attach so much importance to 'the end of 1963'? In 1961 he was a minister, by the end of 1963 he was not.

Mr Enoch Powell is free to make his blood-curdling predictions about the size of the coloured community in this country by the end of the century, although his are the only statistical forecasts which he does not treat with withering contempt. I cannot, however, permit him to rewrite history in order to satisfy his particular whims and fancies of the moment.

Yours faithfully,
HUMPHRY BERKELEY

Mr Powell has never acknowledged or replied to this letter either in private or in public.

At the end of the Third Reading of the Race Relations Bill in 1968, Mr Quintin Hogg, then the Conservative Party's spokesman on Home Office affairs, pledged that a future Conservative Government would work the Act. I rejoined the Conservative Party in 1969. This was a serious error of judgment, but I did not foresee that Mr Heath would face the break-up of the Commonwealth with equanimity in his determination to sell arms to South Africa. Nor did I envisage that Sir Alec Douglas-Home would propose a further round of talks with the Smith regime after the introduction in Rhodesia in 1970 of the new republican constitution which will preserve white minority rule for ever. Nor could I have predicted that a Conservative Government would introduce an Immigrants Bill, despite the protests of the Chairman of the Community Relations Commission and the Police Federation, requiring new Commonwealth immigrants to register with the police. This provision can only have the effect of damaging relations between immigrants and the police.*

I am quite clear as to what Britain's policy should be on immigration and race. First we must acknowledge absolute responsibility for our citizens of Asian origin in East Africa. The raising of the quota from 1,500 a year to 3,000 a year is a welcome step but is not enough. Then we must negotiate with the East African governments their phased entry into this country over an eight- to ten-year period. Many of these people are professional people, often with considerable means; they are highly desirable immigrants in every sense, and their entry into this country would be as beneficial to our society as that of the Huguenots and the Jews in earlier times. Their presence among us would help to rid the British public of the view that poverty and colour are necessarily equated. It is essential that the British public should be made aware of this fallacy as soon as possible, because as coloured children go through our educational system the able ones among them will not expect to become railway porters or bus conductors. Nor should they. In thirty years time in Britain I want to see coloured company directors, judges, professional men, police and army officers. It is the real task of the political parties to prepare the public to expect this to happen as a matter of course.

Already a social problem appears to arise in that Indian and Pakistani children, despite the language difficulties which sometimes exist, appear to be actually brighter than their coloured counterparts from the West Indies. While I think it desirable that our coloured citizens should straddle our complete social structure, I nevertheless think that it is now necessary to undertake detailed research into the causes of this apparent anomaly in order to avoid social strains by the end of the century.

Whether there will be three million or four million coloured people in this country by the end of the century is completely irrelevant. The only conceivable point of issue in Mr Powell's

*Since this was written Mr Maudling tabled an amendment to the legislation which no longer requires new Commonwealth immigrants to register with the police.

frequent forecasts as to the future size of Britain's coloured population centres on whether he decides to advocate compulsory repatriation. A determined policy of repatriation whether voluntary or compulsory will bring untold human misery to people who know no home but Britain. It must be resisted, and intellectually and emotionally destroyed. Britain can set an example to the world in good community relations, and it is in this direction that she must be led.

Chapter 4

The African Story

Are Africans capable of working a democratic system? Are they even fit to govern themselves? These doubts, which have always been felt by traditionalists in this country and have been firmly answered in the negative by Mr Ian Smith and his supporters in Rhodesia, are now entertained by many of those who gave their support to the concept of the wind of change in the early 1960s. Two military coups in Nigeria within seven months followed by a tragic civil war, the mutinies in East Africa in 1964, the creation of Nkrumah's dictatorship in Ghana and its subsequent replacement by a military regime, the overthrow of Obote, and the long agony of the Congo are triumphantly cited by the supporters of the Smith regime as proof of their argument and justification of their cause. These events are viewed with dismay by many of those who supported the granting of independence to African nations.

I suppose that in 1939 it would have been possible to entertain similar doubts about the European races. The existence of Nazi Germany, Fascist Italy and Franco Spain, together with military dictatorships in Poland, Greece, Hungary and Yugoslavia, and a strictly authoritarian regime in Portugal, indicated at least that some of the older civilizations had yet to master the difficult processes of peaceful constitutional change and government by consent. The brutalities of the Spanish Civil War cast doubts, which have yet to be resolved, about the ability of the Spaniards to govern themselves without bloodshed; and the frightening instability of the French Third Republic gave the French people a contempt for party politicians which they have been slow to overcome. The invasion by Russia of Czechoslovakia in 1968 shows that brute force is still the determining factor in Eastern Europe. The military coup in Greece, commonly held to have been the birthplace of parliamentary democracy, shows at least that coups are not confined to the African continent. Nothing which has yet happened in Africa, including Mau Mau, the racial massacres in Burundi and the Sudan, or the violence in Nigeria and the Congo, has equalled the horrors of the gas chambers or the racial persecution of the Jews.

The last fifteen years have seen – except in the case of Portugal – the almost total withdrawal from Africa of European colonial rule. Within that short space of time over thirty African countries have gained sovereign independence. The process south of the Sahara began with Britain's granting of independence to Ghana in 1957; it was completed in 1968 with the transfer of power in the protectorates of southern Africa on the basis of one man one vote.

It was started by Britain and accelerated by General de Gaulle who liquidated the French African Empire (apart from Algeria which followed later), almost overnight. Those who would like to blame Mr Macmillan for his 'wind of change' speech, and Mr Macleod, too, for being the instrument of that policy, should direct their attention to General de Gaulle who proved to be the greatest and swiftest decolonizer of all time.

Perhaps because of the German occupation of France during the war years and perhaps because of the suffering and humiliation of the Indo-China war, the French were able to contemplate the simultaneous lowering of the French flag in a dozen African territories without the introspective heart-searching which gripped the British as each colony moved towards self-government. General de Gaulle certainly saw with severe reality that to govern the Upper Volta in no way added to the glory of France. The fact that African leaders such as Senghor and Houphet Boignet had actually served in French Parliaments and Cabinets ensured that the governments which replaced French rule were not unsympathetic to French aspirations or culture.

The stated objective of British colonial rule, at least in recent years, has been to fit the inhabitants of colonial territories for self-government, and then to withdraw. Yet it is difficult to think of any common criteria which can have led Britain to grant independence to Ghana in 1957, to Kenya in 1963 and to Bechuanaland in 1966. There were and are no comparable minimum standards of education, wealth or contact with the West, between the territories. Nor did the Colonial Office in 1957 envisage that its task in Africa would have been completed within ten years, or even within the foreseeable future.

In recent years I have come to question whether alien rule can ever make an indigenous population fit to govern itself or still less judge with any accuracy when the moment for self-government has arrived. The developed countries can assist in the provision of technical assistance and educational opportunities and training programmes but these do not cease with independence; on the contrary they are accelerated. To ask whether the Nigerians or the Congolese are capable of governing themselves in 1971 is for me a question as meaningless and unanswerable as whether the French were capable of so doing at the time of the French Revolution.

In fact, despite the undoubted material benefits of colonial rule, particularly since 1945, the British withdrew from Africa, not because commonly agreed standards of political and economic maturity had been attained in each territory one by one, but because domestic public opinion would not stomach the imposition of indefinite British rule by force of arms on an unwilling population. This was last attempted by Britain in Ireland in the early 1920s and by France in Algeria. In both cases defeat was inevitable and the bloodshed was both unnecessary and appalling.

In justice to British colonial rule, once the decision was taken that it was unacceptable to rule by force indefinitely, and once the formula of fitness to rule, however loosely thought out, was evolved, a hurried attempt was made to plant British political institutions and the Westminster pattern of democracy on African soil. I do not criticize this decision. It is difficult enough for any nation to evolve a system of government by consent, and as a nation we could only attempt to teach other peoples what we ourselves had learned over centuries of practice. But we should not have been as surprised as we were that this attempt was not altogether successful.

We must understand that until a few years before independence, rule in each British colonial territory was frankly authoritarian. Emergency rule, detention without trial, restriction and even deportation were widely practised. Dr Nkrumah, Mr Kenyatta, Dr Kaunda and Dr Banda were all, in their day, victims of these arbitrary processes. Two or three years of a Parliament, a Speaker and a Mace were inevitably an insufficient preparation for enduring rule on the Westminster pattern. There was something supremely ironic in asking Dr Banda to agree to a Bill of Rights in the Malawi Independence Constitution only two years after he had been released from a period of fifteen months' detention without trial.

We should also realize that the Westminster pattern of democracy contains two features which are not wholly appropriate for an African society in which liberty is to be preserved. First, there is the absolute sovereignty of Parliament, and secondly, there is the practical necessity – if it is to work smoothly – of a two-party system with the opposition as the alternative government. It was the unfettered power of Parliament together with the collapse of any effective opposition which enabled Dr Nkrumah to set up his ugly dictatorship quite legally. It was the universal nature of independence movements which frustrated the emergence of opposition parties unless these were tribalist in origin. While it would be wrong to dogmatize, it is now becoming clear that for most African countries a presidential form of government is required, with strong executive powers.

The absence of effective opposition parties does not necessarily mean the withering away of democracy. To quote Julius Nyerere:

> The Nationalist movement which fights for and achieves independence inevitably forms the government of the new state. It would surely be ridiculous to expect that a country should voluntarily divide itself for the sake of conforming to a particular expression of democracy and to do so during a struggle which calls for the complete unity of its people. No one should jump to the conclusion that such a country is not democratic or does not intend to be democratic.

Accepting that Tanganyika (as it was then called) was a *de facto* one-party state at the time of independence in 1961, in the sense that in free elections no other party gained any parliamentary representation, Nyerere argued that the Westminster pattern and the two-party system were a positive invitation to tyranny. So long as Tanganyika remained in theory a multi-party state, TANU, the ruling party, could field only one candidate in each constituency. Because the splinter parties were short of funds and organizational skills, and because of the absence of genuine issues on which to fight and the lack of popular backing, many if not all the constituencies would remain uncontested. Hence the electors would be deprived of a genuine choice. Once elected the Members of Parliament would be subjected to the two-party discipline which is a feature of Westminster, even though they faced no actual opponents in the Chamber. Thus, controversy was confined to private meetings of the TANU parliamentary group, and in public Parliament rubber-stamped the decisions which had been taken in private by the TANU parliamentary group which in practice was identical in terms of membership to Parliament as a whole. In this way, party discipline of a kind approved by the British party organizations and the Whips at Westminster created, in the absence of a genuine political enemy, that very lack of choice and airing of controversy in public upon which political freedom depends.

To avoid the danger, Nyerere and his supporters decided to establish a *de jure* one-party state in Tanzania. TANU, the only party, was there for all Tanzanian citizens to join. Once the theoretical intervention of other parties at the polls was eliminated, it became possible for more than one TANU candidate to stand in each constituency. In the General Election of 1965 two TANU candidates fought each other in each constituency: forty members of the previous Parliament, including nine ministers, were defeated and thus a genuine choice was offered to the electors. One of the most remarkable features of this election was the return of an Englishman, Derek Bryceson, with a majority of 30,000 over his African opponent. Elections were again held in 1970 and Derek Bryceson and Amir Jamal the Finance Minister (an Asian) were re-elected, defeating their African opponents. In the Tanzanian Parliament the system of whipping has now been abolished; all legislation is decided by a free vote. If a measure is beaten it is withdrawn. The only discipline to which Members of Parliament are subjected is the threat of dissolution if a measure considered vital by the Government fails to get through. By this means President Nyerere has tried to link the one-party state to a genuine freedom of choice which could not in his view have been maintained by the continuation of the British parliamentary system.

Because we have attempted to export our form of parliamentary government to Africa, lock, stock and barrel, too often people in Britain are dismayed when this is altered and adapted to fit local needs. Instead, I suggest, we should recognize that the form of government which the Anglo-Saxon race has evolved over centuries of usage may well be unsuitable for an African state which is in a different state of development with a different social hierarchy. We should also recognize that the adaptations and alterations which will be made to our cherished exported institutions in such countries as Kenya, Zambia and Tanzania may result in a democracy which is no less authentic.

Up to now I have talked about British colonies in Africa which do not have substantial settler minorities. Once the British Government decided that to maintain rule by force was impossible, their way ahead has been clear. The vain attempt to establish defined criteria as to a colony's fitness for self-government inevitably meant disputes over the timing for constitutional advance. Events elsewhere in Africa played a more decisive role in determining the actual timetable. No one doubted that before the British withdrew, a government would have been established which Britain tried to ensure would be in conformity with the wishes of the majority of the inhabitants of the territories concerned. But in Central Africa the ultimate solution was far less obvious.

Since 1923, Southern Rhodesia has been governed by a small white settler minority. For ten years, from 1953 to 1963, an attempt was made to extend this settler rule to the now independent countries of Zambia and Malawi. The concept of the Federation of Rhodesia and Nyasaland was not ignoble. British Governments hoped that by joining the racialist state of

Southern Rhodesia to the British protectorates of Northern Rhodesia and Nyasaland, more liberal racial practices would prevail in Southern Rhodesia and extreme black nationalism would be avoided in the Northern Territories. The experiment failed because the politicians from Salisbury who dominated the Federation for far too long, preached partnership and practised apartheid. But, until the publication of the Monckton Report in 1960, it was hoped in Salisbury and feared in the Northern Territories that the aim of the British Government was to grant sovereign independence to a Federation governed by a white minority.

Such an outcome would not have been possible without violence in Africa and prolonged controversy and bitter opposition at home. Once it was clear that Tanganyika, Kenya and Uganda were to join Ghana, Nigeria and Sierra Leone as independent countries with majority rule, it was clear that the same principles must apply to Malawi and Zambia. This took effect in 1964, when Rhodesia remained a self-governing colony under white rule with a status just technically short of sovereign independence. If Britain had given legal independence to this white minority, she would have contradicted the entire basis of her post-war colonial policy.

The motives of the white Rhodesians are mixed. Some are genuinely attempting to formulate objective criteria (which everybody has failed to do) as to the fitness of Africans to vote and thus participate in ruling—hence the talk about majority rule in ten or fifteen years' time. Others, who form the majority, are determined to maintain white rule for ever. The composition of the white Rhodesian population is mixed: some are genuine Rhodesians who know no other home; many, perhaps a majority, are post-war immigrants from Britain or South Africa, often artisans who have gone to Rhodesia for a higher standard of living than they could obtain anywhere else. Their way of life is threatened by African advance, for they are paid ten times as much as an African for jobs which Africans are quite capable of filling. Just as Britain had to recognize that she could not rule an alien population indefinitely by force, so I believe that the white Rhodesians will be forced to the same conclusion in the end. Just as Britain in practice recognized that there can be no criteria as to fitness to rule, so in time the white Rhodesians who use this argument to justify their rebellion must recognize that there is no basic difference between Africans in Zambia and Africans in Rhodesia. At this point it will become clear that the sole impediment to African political advance in Rhodesia is a white settler population of a quarter of a million people, about 5 per cent of the population of the country.

That there is a place for the white man in Africa is shown in Zambia, Malawi, Tanzania and Kenya. However, I must make clear the type of European and the circumstances in which he will be welcome. For the foreseeable future the local chief executives of large international institutions such as Shell, Unilever, or Anglo American will be white, as will some of their senior staff. But these are not settlers. European settlers are actually encouraged to retire in Kenya provided that they can support themselves, although they cannot buy freehold land. I doubt whether the big farmer has a long-term future in East or Central Africa, where there is a shortage of good cultivatable land. I see no future for the bulk of Mr Ian Smith's supporters many of whom are semi-skilled or unskilled artisans. They are in jobs which could perfectly well be filled by unemployed Africans and are so filled in Zambia. They are standing in the way of African advance and they should never have gone to Rhodesia where they live a middle-class life on working-class skills. Their behaviour will inevitably affect the fate and security of their kith and kin in the independent countries of Black Africa. It may be that a future British Government will have to compensate them financially to make them leave Rhodesia—for leave they must.

I do not believe that majority rule – or one man one vote (there is no valid distinction between the two) – would be disastrous in Rhodesia any more than it has been in other countries. Paradoxically, an African Nationalist government in Rhodesia would almost certainly produce a ministry containing more university graduates than that of Mr Smith. The bitterness between the races may make necessary a longer period of transitional rule.

I have already stated that no meaningful negotiation could

take place between the British Government and the Smith regime. I further stated that a real settlement could only be achieved if representatives of the African Nationalist parties participate in any negotiations that may be held. In the absence of any genuine settlement, and so long as the rebellion in Rhodesia lasts, I must give my moral support to the freedom-fighters in Rhodesia. Though I am a man of peace, and warfare is abhorrent to me, I am not a pacifist. Since the African majority in Rhodesia is denied any means of constitutional redress by the European minority, because it does not have proper access to the ballot box, it is driven to strive for justice through revolutionary means. I regard African freedom-fighters as being on precisely the same footing as any member of the resistance movements in Europe during the years of Nazi occupation. The agreement reached between Sir Alec Douglas-Home and Mr Ian Smith on 24th November 1971 is an unmitigated disaster. It is a document but not a settlement of the Rhodesian problems. It places Britain firmly but wrongly on the side of White supremacy in Southern Africa. I hope to work within the Labour Party for this situation to be fully recognized and for the African cause to be supported by the next Labour Government.

In his inaugural address William Henry Harrison declared in 1841: 'The only legitimate right to govern is an express grant of power from the Governed.' The British have practised this maxim and the Commonwealth has survived. If the white Rhodesians are allowed to ignore it, they will destroy themselves, they will threaten the existence of the white man elsewhere in Africa, and they will imperil the future of the Commonwealth.

Chapter 5

The Commonwealth Link

For the first time, following the January 1971 Commonwealth Prime Ministers' meeting in Singapore, I sense among thoughtful people in this country more than just a sense of regret that the Commonwealth may disintegrate. Now I sense also a genuine introspective heart-searching about the value of the Commonwealth relationship, extending into a scrutiny as to whether the Commonwealth is the sort of body to which Britain ought to belong. In a sense the people of Britain are now undergoing the same doubts which have been felt in many individual Commonwealth countries in the post-war period; though these doubts stem from diametrically opposed analyses of the nature of the Commonwealth.

The new Commonwealth countries have tended to regard the Commonwealth as an essentially British institution. Though the transfer of sovereignty has invariably taken place in an atmosphere of good will and – with few exceptions – has always been accompanied by Commonwealth membership, newly independent nations have frequently regarded disagreement with current British policy as being a perfectly valid reason for threatening to leave the Commonwealth. There were such moves in India at the time of Suez, and more recently when Britain appeared to India to be unduly sympathetic to Pakistan during the fighting in 1965. The threat by Presidents Kaunda and Nyerere to leave the Commonwealth if Britain were to resume the sale of arms to South Africa has its earlier precedents.

At the very time when African and Asian countries still relate British policy and action to their own Commonwealth membership, thus emphasizing their strictly bilateral view of the Commonwealth relationship, the British people have come to regard the Commonwealth as being essentially Afro-Asian in outlook. Many of them do not wish to be part of an organization which in their view appears to have so decisive and even harmful an influence on British policy. Many of them resent what they regard as diplomatic blackmail by other Commonwealth countries. It is this misunderstanding on both sides that has led to the 1971 Commonwealth crisis.

The nature of the Commonwealth underwent a fundamental change in the immediate post-war period. The Statute of Westminster had defined the relationship of the United Kingdom and the Dominions as 'Autonomous communities within the British Empire, equal in status, in no way subordinate one to another in any aspect of their domestic or external relations, though united by a common allegiance to the Crown, and freely associated as members of the British Commonwealth of Nations.' This definition was both precise and accurate. The heart of the relationship was a common allegiance to a single Crown.

Even during the 1930s small but significant changes in the relationship occurred. Canada and South Africa inaugurated diplomatic missions of their own, which King George V at the time thought endangered the concept of a single Crown. Relations between the Dominions and the United Kingdom began to be conducted through High Commissioners rather than through the Governors-General.

A further test came at the outbreak of World War II. Australia and New Zealand assumed that the declaration of war against Germany made in His Majesty's name by the United Kingdom Government automatically meant that they too were at war with Germany. Canada and South Africa both called meetings of their own parliaments to declare war on Germany, and in the case of South Africa this declaration was only carried by a small parliamentary majority. Eire, which in practice had ceased to be regarded as a dominion, remained neutral. The decision of Canada and South Africa that they were not bound by a declaration made on behalf of His Majesty by the British Government was a direct challenge to the unity of the Crown, and although both countries entered the war, the theory then had to be accepted that the King of the United

Kingdom might be at war when the King of Canada and the King of South Africa might be neutral.

The change which was to have the most far-reaching effect on the nature of the Commonwealth was the decision that India could remain in the Commonwealth, recognizing the King as its head, after she became a Republic in 1950. Not only was this a constitutional change of the greatest importance, but for the first time, with the accession of India, Pakistan and Ceylon – all avowedly non-committed countries – to Commonwealth membership, practical recognition was given to the fact that the Commonwealth no longer attempted to pursue a common foreign policy.

Although this transformation of the composition of the Commonwealth was, of course, recognized in Whitehall, it was not grasped for many years by the British public. Nor did the politicians feel it necessary to enlighten the public in this respect. As the process of de-colonization gained speed with the granting of independence to Ghana and Malaya in 1957, and to eighteen other territories in Africa, the Mediterranean and the Caribbean by 1970, the fact that each country remained within the Commonwealth both dulled the blow of the vanishing of the Empire and helped to give a false picture of the future relationship between Britain and its former dependencies.

It can be argued that the Commonwealth played a valuable role in this period by disguising from the colonels of Cheltenham the fact that the Empire was being liquidated, and thus preventing the wars of colonial retreat which the French suffered in Indo-China and Algeria. But it was, for this reason, not sufficiently recognized that the transfer of power was not from the Colonial Office to the Commonwealth Relations Office but from London to Lagos, Kuala Lumpur and Dar-es-Salaam. Hence the obsessive concern of the British with subsequent political developments in their former colonies compared to the indifference with which, for example, they regarded political instability in Latin America or elsewhere.

Although successive British Governments recognized the fundamental changes which had occurred in the Commonwealth in the post-war period, little effort was made to form into an organic whole what was in fact a series of bilateral relationships between this country and its former dependencies. Relations between Britain and other Commonwealth countries continued to be handled by the Commonwealth Relations Office, even though the common foreign policy of the pre-war period had ceased to exist. The last ten years have seen major international crises which have affected individual Commonwealth countries – for example, Cyprus, Malaysia, India and Pakistan twice – and now we have the Rhodesia problem, and the proposal by Mr Heath's Government to sell maritime arms to South Africa.

None of these crises is strictly a Commonwealth matter. The Cyprus problem is essentially a difference between Greece and Turkey; it is of NATO concern and of cold-war importance but its effect on the Commonwealth is minimal. Similarly the confrontation between Indonesia and Malaysia has been a secondary power struggle in South-East Asia, of significance to other powers in that area who may only incidentally be Commonwealth members.

The protracted dispute between India and Pakistan over Kashmir has made its contribution towards Commonwealth evolution only because it has shown that Commonwealth countries which are neighbours can disagree violently, and even fight each other, while remaining within the organization. Pakistan and Nigeria are unhappy examples of the fact that Commonwealth countries are not immune from the tragedy of civil war. Even the Rhodesian crisis and the proposed arms sales, which have threatened to break up the Commonwealth, have their wider implications involving the OAU and the United Nations. They have assumed a Commonwealth importance because in each case Britain has a direct responsibility, and Britain is the one country in the Commonwealth with whom each other country has had at one time a colonial relationship.

From 1961 until 1968 when the amalgamation took place I argued that one Department of External Affairs should conduct our overseas policy both with foreign and Commonwealth countries. Indeed in 1964 I initiated a debate in the House of Commons and advocated this. I was opposed by the front bench of both parties. After the war, the former Commonwealth Office had to perform two difficult and often incompatible functions. First it was responsible for diplomatic dealings between Britain and other sovereign Commonwealth countries in matters which frequently had wider than Commonwealth implications. Secondly, in the absence until 1965 of any Commonwealth Secretariat, it acted as the functional link which kept the Commonwealth together. The first role became increasingly irrelevant as each Commonwealth country pursued its own separate foreign policy. The second role perpetuated the notion that the Commonwealth was peculiarly British, and this in turn has led to the belief that an unresolved quarrel between Britain and another Commonwealth country could and should logically lead to a withdrawal by that country from the Commonwealth. In fact, on grounds of strict logic, there is more justification in President Kaunda's suggestion of expelling Britain from the Commonwealth.

I must now try to describe what the Commonwealth in fact is, recognizing considerable failure both in Britain and many other Commonwealth countries to comprehend how it has developed in recent years. The only common factor is that all Commonwealth countries were once governed by Britain. As a result of this former state of dependency three other institutions have evolved which include most, but not all Commonwealth countries, and which in some cases go beyond the Commonwealth. These are the Sterling Area, the Ottawa Preference Area and the British Aid Programme. All Commonwealth countries except Canada are in the first, although it includes non-Commonwealth countries such as South Africa, Ireland and Kuwait. The system of Imperial Preference still includes South Africa. Most African Commonwealth countries do not give preference to British goods and derive little benefit from the preference that Britain offers.

Over 80 per cent of Britain's aid programme goes to underdeveloped Commonwealth countries. None of these institutions would necessarily alter if the Commonwealth were to break up, nor would any country at present in the Commonwealth necessarily lose any advantages which it gains from these institutions if it were to leave the Commonwealth, though if

Britain joins the European Community the Sterling Area will ultimately go, as will Commonwealth preference. The most important feature of the British Aid Programme is the provision of skilled manpower under the Overseas Service Aid Programme. The continuance of this form of aid must depend upon the willingness of people to serve in particular countries overseas; many might be reluctant to do so if the Commonwealth link were to be cut. From this it is clear that the formal strands which bind the Commonwealth together hardly exist, and some of the benefits which historically derive from Commonwealth membership could be maintained after the Commonwealth had ceased to exist, and Britain had joined the Community. If this be so, say the cynics or the disillusioned, why needlessly prolong the patient's life?

First, let us look at Britain's position in severely practical terms. It is probably no loger true that Britain's role as the centre of the Commonwealth adds to her prestige or her influence as a world power. It is, however, true that the Commonwealth can no longer be the stumbling-block which might prevent Britain from joining the European Community, since many Commonwealth States have been offered associated status, and special provision has been made for the products of others. Though the irritation which many British people feel at Commonwealth pressure for a just end to the Rhodesian rebellion is understandable, it is irrational. With the exception of South Africa, the end of British colonial rule in each former colony has involved the transfer of power to a government which represents the majority of the people of the territory. The South African precedent was not encouraging. Whether or not the Commonwealth was there to exert pressure, the British Government would be morally bound to grant legal independence to Rhodesia only in circumstances and under conditions which were acceptable to the people of Rhodesia as a whole. It is quite clear that the Smith regime does not command this acceptance. It is equally clear that the prime aim of the Smith regime is to perpetuate white minority rule indefinitely. No agreement that could be reached with the Smith regime, in the light of recent events, would be acceptable to British domestic opinion. The same pressures which the Commonwealth Prime

Ministers exert on Britain to intensify the measures against the Smith regime have in any event been applied at the United Nations and from within Parliament itself. Even though the present Conservative Government was committed – largely for domestic political pre-election purposes – to a further round of talks with the Smith regime, Sir Alec Douglas-Home said in public a little while ago that he did not rate the possibility of a successful outcome of the negotiations as higher than one chance in a hundred.

I have so far considered the negative side of Britain's membership of the Commonwealth. Although an island race, the British have never been insular in their outlook. The colonial Empire provided an outlet for service abroad; the Commonwealth provides a similar outlet for a different form of service. The District Commissioner and the Governor have all but disappeared but there is urgent need in Commonwealth countries for doctors, teachers and engineers. The OSAS scheme is the channel for this need. It is now becoming clear that racialism is the greatest single danger in the way of peaceful development: Britain's relations through the Commonwealth with peoples of all races and all continents should prevent the cult in Britain of a narrow racialism which runs counter to all our past history. The existence of the Commonwealth and Britain's membership of it undoubtedly made the original Commonwealth Immigrants Act of 1962 a more civilized and humane measure than it would otherwise have been. The Commonwealth has helped Britain to remain an outward-looking nation—although the East African Asian Act, the present immigration legislation, and Mr Heath's stated determination not to be pushed around by his fellow Commonwealth Prime Ministers indicate a narrower view of Britain's national interests than would have been thought possible six years ago.

There are also strong reasons why the new members of the Commonwealth should wish the institution to continue. For the most part they are small countries, they need capital and technical assistance and, often, military aid. Naturally, they instinctively turn to those whom they know and understand for this provision—in this case to other members of the Commonwealth, mainly Britain but increasingly Canada and Australia. Most of them are deeply conscious of racial tensions. In many African countries the indigenous population were until recently treated as second-class citizens; they were denied political rights and they were the victims of racial discrimination. The advent of independence has made them masters in their own house, but with commendable restraint they have not practised racial discrimination in reverse against the white settler communities in their countries. They have joined the Commonwealth as free and equal partners where they sit with people whom hitherto they were forced to regard as their masters. It is this non-racial aspect of the Commonwealth which Kenneth Kaunda has many times told me that he prizes most about his membership, and this is what he most fears will be jeopardized if racialism were to triumph in Rhodesia. It was for this reason that the withdrawal of South Africa from the Commonwealth ten years ago was necessary if the Commonwealth were to survive, and it is for this reason that the sale of arms to the practitioners of apartheid has again brought its survival into question. While Britain, in my judgment, behaved with dishonour in betraying her nationals of Asian origin in East Africa, I must state that the East African countries of Kenya, Uganda and Tanzania have not always shown tolerance towards those of their own citizens who are Asians. In particular, the Tanzanian nationalization of personal property without compensation, though justified as socialism, is unhappily racialist in effect and will inevitably impoverish the Asian community in that country.

My conclusion is that it is in the interests of Britain and the Commonwealth as a whole for great efforts to be made to prevent the Commonwealth's dissolution. It can only continue if reality is substituted for mythology. Britain must recognize that it is not the Empire under another name and that, while the relationship is no doubt special, the essence of special relationships is that it is not necessary to refer to them. The newer Commonwealth countries must recognize that the Commonwealth is not Britain's preserve, and that it should not be used as a bargaining weapon every time Britain's policies come under criticism. The creation of the Commonwealth Secretariat, which emphasizes the fact that Britain no longer runs the Commonwealth, was long overdue. It should be used constructively to bring added life to other institutions such as the Commonwealth Parliamentary Association. There is much to be said for moving the headquarters of the Secretariat from London to another capital (possibly Ottawa), since the greatest need is to create links between other Commonwealth countries in addition to the close ties which they will always have with Britain. The advantages of rotating the meeting-place for Commonwealth Prime Ministers' Conferences – which I advocated in 1966 – are now obvious.

I hope that even those who see little point in perpetuating the Commonwealth recognize that it would be a tragedy if it were to dissolve over the question of Rhodesia or the sale by Britain of arms to South Africa. This would be a severe blow for all who are working towards racial harmony. I hope that those who see the Rhodesia crisis or the arms issue as a means of getting rid of the coloured members of the Commonwealth will come to recognize that a purely white Commonwealth, of the type which many white Rhodesians would wish to join, would increase racial tension in the world.

Unlike the United Nations, the Commonwealth would not have to be invented if it did not exist already. It is an historical accident. If it were to wither and eventually die through lack of mutual interest or the will to keep it going, many people, including myself, would feel a sadness comparable to the death of a relative. If it were to be torn apart because of the obstinacy of a British Prime Minister in advancing dishonest reasons for giving Dr Vorster his certificate of respectability, Britain would, I feel, become a less civilized place in which to live.

Chapter 6

The United Nations

In November 1966 I became Chairman of the United Nations Association of Great Britain and Northern Ireland at the unanimous wish of the members of the National Executive Committee. I was not a newcomer to UNA. From 1962 until 1964 I had been honorary secretary of the United Nations Parliamentary Group. My father had worked on the staff of the League of Nations Union before his election to Parliament, and before that was one of the original members of the League Secretariat. I remained Chairman of UNA until April 1970. I do not wish to write about the internal disagreements which occurred towards the end of my chairmanship beyond saying that at all times I acted in what seemed to be the best interests of the Association and its members.

Although the post of Chairman of UNA is voluntary and unpaid I found that the duties consumed at least half of each working day. I had access, on matters affecting Britain and the United Nations (a very wide spectrum), to Foreign Office Ministers, the Foreign Secretary and even, on occasion, to the Prime Minister. In the course of several visits which I made to the United Nations Headquarters (at my own expense), I came to know well U Thant, senior members of the UN Secretariat and, in particular, Lord Caradon with whom I stayed on a number of occasions. Lord Caradon, who held ministerial rank as a member of the Government, acquired a remarkable and well-earned reputation. He represented Britain for five difficult years after the illegal declaration of independence in Rhodesia, yet his position was unrivalled. I regret the fact that Mr Heath's Government has reverted to the previous practice of appointing a career diplomat as Britain's Permanent Representative at the UN. There is no doubt that a senior minister who has direct access to the Prime Minister can speak with greater authority both on Britain's behalf in New York and to his ministerial colleagues at home.

No international organization has been the subject of greater misunderstanding than the United Nations. People often talk about handing over a problem to the UN, or they criticize the UN for failing to act in a particular situation. I often received letters from people asking how I could go on supporting the UN after the disgraceful vote on Gibraltar. Such people talk about the UN as though it were a sovereign power. They rarely seemed to understand that it is merely an instrument which can be used to maintain world peace, or grow rusty and even get thrown away. Of course, I deplored the fact that so many member states should have so forgotten the basic principles relating to self-determination which are enshrined in the Charter, as to have voted that Gibraltar should be returned to Spain in contravention of the clear wishes of its people. No supporter of the UN has to approve of every vote of the General Assembly, let alone the votes of individual member states. I am a supporter of parliamentary government, but this does not mean that I support necessarily the votes of particular parliaments or the speeches and conduct of particular Members of Parliament.

It should be recognized that the United Nations was established in 1945 as an instrument for the preservation of peace and it has such powers and resources as its members care to give it. On several occasions since 1945 it has been used effectively by its members to prevent fighting and to stop a small war from escalating. There have also been cases when it has not been so used, and slaughter on a horrifying scale has taken place—most notably in Nigeria, Vietnam and Pakistan. It is fair to say, however, that the seemingly endless talks between the Americans and the North Vietnamese were brought about through the personal initiative of U Thant.

There have been at least three occasions since 1945 when the United Nations has been used with some success as an instrument for peacekeeping and peacemaking, and carried out a function that no other body could have performed. Peacekeeping involves the use of UN military personnel to stop fighting or to prevent fighting in a particular area. Peacemaking is the complementary function of mediation, and the resolution of disputes through discussion, with the aim of making the peacekeeping operation no longer necessary.

Apart from the Korean war, which is untypical because it happened during a period when the Soviet Union was boycotting the Security Council, the most successful UN peacekeeping and peacemaking operation took place in the Congo. In 1960 the Congo, a country about the size of India with a population of fourteen million and only a dozen university graduates, was granted independence by Belgium. Within a fortnight the army had mutinied against its Belgian officers; and shortly afterwards the Belgian army officers and civil servants were withdrawn, except from the copper-rich province of Katanga which – under Moise Tshombe, its provincial President – illegally declared that it had seceded from the Congo. At the request of the President and Prime Minister of the Congo, the United Nations set up the largest military and civilian operation that it has so far undertaken.

The achievements of the UN were threefold. Firstly, the territorial integrity of the Congo was maintained and the Congo is a unified country today. It could have fragmented into at least four segments. Secondly, the cold war was kept out of that part of Africa: it is easy to envisage that a situation similar to that in Vietnam might otherwise have developed. Thirdly, the UN provided the civilian infrastructure to enable the vast country to be administered.

It seemed to me at the time that the British Conservative Government, while paying lip service to supporting the United Nations operation in the Congo, nevertheless secretly sympathized with Tshombe's desire to secede. I paid a visit to the Congo in January 1963 and – in a speech I made in the House of Commons shortly afterwards – was able to dispel stories of atrocities which the Katanga Lobby alleged had been committed by UN troops. I had a double satisfaction. A personal note was passed up to my seat from Mr Peter Thomas, then Minister of State at the Foreign Office, which said 'many congratulations on a truly magnificent speech'. Mr Christopher Mayhew, who wound up for the Opposition, said 'If the Hon.

Member for Lancaster [Mr Berkeley] were the Secretary of State for Foreign Affairs the prestige of the Government would rise not only in this country but perhaps in some of the countries where, as he rightly said, the Government have lost a great deal of good will and prestige for Britain by their action in the Congo crisis.' I visited the Congo again in December 1968 and in retrospect the magnitude of the UN operation had become obvious. The Congo is now peaceful and will shortly be among the richest countries in Africa.

In January 1964 civil war broke out on the island of Cyprus. By April 1964, despite some initial resistance from the British Government, a United Nations peacekeeping force was established in Cyprus. Again, the instrument of the UN was rightly used since no other body could have kept the peace, either on the island or between Greece and Turkey. Cyprus is only forty miles from the Turkish mainland; its population is 82 per cent Greek and only 18 per cent Turkish. Had the machinery of the UN not been used Turkey would have invaded Cyprus. Greece would have retaliated and war would have broken out between two NATO allies. I regretted the reluctance of the British Government to use the UN machinery since I did not see how British troops alone could successfully be used on a long-term basis to keep the peace in what had been only a few years earlier a turbulent British colony.

In May 1964 I visited Greece, Cyprus and Turkey. I had talks with the Greek and Turkish Prime Ministers and in Cyprus with President Makarios, Dr Kutchuk the Vice President and with the UN Mediator and the UN Force Commander. I found that there was a complete breakdown in relations between the two communities on the island. To travel from Nicosia to Kyrenia I had to pass nine separate armed roadblocks, eight of them illegally manned by Turks with sten guns, and one near Kyrenia manned by armed Greek Cypriot irregulars. At each road block UN troops were also stationed. When I travelled from the Ledra Palace Hotel to see Dr Kutchuk in his house in Nicosia I had to drive myself because no taxi driver from the Greek quarter was prepared to chance his life in the Turkish quarter.

I spoke in the House of Commons on my return and advocated a strengthening of the UN mandate, including the right of the UN to impose a political settlement if necessary. Harold Wilson – then Leader of the Opposition – was kind enough to refer in his winding-up speech, to 'an extremely interesting speech from the Hon. Member for Lancaster (Mr Berkeley) on the problem of the position of British troops and the conditions under which we should be prepared to stay in Cyprus'. Re-reading my speech after an interval of seven years I believe I was right to say that pacification was an indispensable pre-requisite to a political settlement, and on the peacekeeping side the UN operation has been highly successful. I have visited Cyprus twice in 1971; there is still a UN force of three thousand men but for the most part the road blocks have gone and the killing has stopped. On the peacemaking side little if any progress has taken place. There have been successive UN Mediators, the latest of whom (Mr Osorio Taffal) has been in Cyprus for three years. With his encouragement, talks have been held between the leaders of the Greek Cypriots and the leaders of the Turkish Cypriots during most of this time. Yet a political settlement is no nearer. If the UN force were to be withdrawn we should be back to the position which existed in 1964. The presence of three thousand UN troops in Cyprus may be a small price to pay to avoid a civil war in Cyprus and war between Greece and Turkey. Yet as long as the UN is in Cyprus nobody feels the urgent need to reach a political settlement, and this is why, in 1964, I asked the British Government to advocate in the Security Council a stronger mandate, including the power to impose a settlement. I maintain this view because the alternative is for a UN contingent to remain in Cyprus indefinitely.

A more controversial area in which the United Nations has been almost continuously involved for more than twenty years is the Middle East. Its ten-year period of peacekeeping from 1957 until 1967 has been forgotten and the Six-Day War of 1967 is more widely remembered. Few decisions have been more misrepresented than U Thant's decision to withdraw the United Nations Emergency Force at the request of President Nasser in May 1967. Two myths have grown up, both of which are equally inaccurate, even though they have both at different times been subscribed to by Sir Alec Douglas-Home. The first is that if U Thant had refused to accede to President Nasser's request the Middle East war could have been averted. The second is that President Nasser was bluffing and that he was more surprised than anybody else when his demands were met. I discussed the matter in the greatest detail with U Thant, Ralph Bunche and Major-General Rikhye (the Commander of UNEF), in New York in August 1967.

The Egyptian Government's request for the withdrawal of UNEF from the Sinai peninsular reached General Rikhye at 22.00 hrs. on 16 May 1967. It was made clear to him that this request covered the UNEF contingent at Sharm-el-Sheikh which dominates the Straits of Tiran. General Rikhye replied that he had no authority to deal with a request of this nature, and the request was then transmitted to U Thant through the proper channels, reaching him in New York at noon on 18 May. By the morning of 17 May Egyptian forces had surrounded three United Nations observation posts, including El Sabha and had also arrived by helicopter at Sharm-el-Sheikh with an order for the United Nations contingent of thirty-two men to vacate their post within fifteen minutes, a time limit that was subsequently amended to forty-eight hours. UNEF had no mandate to fire on Egyptian troops on Egyptian soil. The military advice to U Thant from General Rikhye, which he repeated to me in August 1967 was, that in the light of these events, UNEF had already ceased to be able to perform the functions for which it had been set up, namely to interpose between Egyptian and Israeli forces.

These Egyptian troop movements in themselves largely dispose of the myth that President Nasser was bluffing about UNEF's withdrawal. However, U Thant immediately cabled Mr Mahmud Riad, the Egyptian Foreign Minister, announced his intention of visiting President Nasser and expressed the hope that the request for the withdrawal of UNEF would itself be withdrawn. In reply he was informed that while he would be personally welcome, if he persisted in his attempt to bring about a change of mind he would receive 'a stern rebuff'. In the meantime, India and Yugoslavia, whose units comprised nearly half the total strength of UNEF, informed the

Secretary-General that they would in any event withdraw their men from UNEF. The legal position was even clearer: UNEF's position rested on an exchange of letters between Mr Dag Hammarskjöld and President Nasser which expressly stated the UNEF could only remain on Egyptian soil with the consent of the host country.

U Thant has been criticized for not immediately calling a meeting of the Security Council. This would not, of course, have removed the practical problem that UNEF's role had been destroyed by the Egyptian army movements. Since, however, the Security Council was in any event immobilized by Soviet action between 25 May and 5 June it must be very doubtful whether it could have acted decisively if it had been summoned. The storm of abuse that was levelled towards U Thant, including references to 'U Thant's war', let off the real culprits somewhat too easily. As the Secretary-General himself said, 'the basis for UNEF was essentially fragile'.

The instrument failed to stop the Six-Day War. But the Security Council met and ordered both sides to obey a cease-fire order, thus bringing the fighting to an end without the formal humiliation of a surrender by the Arab states. Without this face-saving formula the Arab states might have requested and received military help from their friends in the Eastern bloc.

Since then the UN instrument has been used through the medium of Ambassador Jarring's mission to grope towards a permanent Middle East peace-settlement. Although peace may be a long way off, few can doubt that it can only be achieved under the UN umbrella and that when and if attained it will be necessary to have a UN presence to patrol both sides of any frontiers that may be agreed.

The tragic events in East Pakistan involving the slaughter of thousands of people and the flight of millions of people from East Pakistan into India has provoked many people to ask what the United Nations could do to mitigate the tragedy. There are two problems of the greatest magnitude: one humanitarian and the other political. On the first: by June 1971, 34 million dollars had been promised by a number of member states and was being channelled through the office of the High

Commissioner for Refugees on the spot. This office was designated by U Thant as the umbrella under which the UN family of organizations would work. Two separate operations were being carried out: relief in East Pakistan; relief and, where appropriate, repatriation, in India. Several voluntary charitable organizations, notably OXFAM, criticized the Secretary-General for observing 'diplomatic niceties' by working through Pakistan Government channels in East Pakistan. Unfortunately, charitable bodies do not always understand political and military realities. In June 1971 East Pakistan was occupied by troops from West Pakistan. Had the UN refused to work through the authorities of the legal Government of Pakistan it would have been expelled from East Pakistan, thus making the plight of the suffering masses in East Pakistan even worse, at least in the short term.

The political problem, unlike relief, is a matter for the Security Council. Charges of genocide have been levelled at the Government of Pakistan, charges which, if true, would mean that Pakistan was in breach of a Convention to which she was a signatory, and that her Government had been guilty of a grave international crime. These charges must be investigated. Although the United Nations Charter precludes interference in matters within the internal juridiction of member states, this provision can be overruled if the Security Council decides that there is a threat to peace. Such a situation clearly existed in June 1971 with the possibility of an outbreak of fighting between India and Pakistan, which has now happened.

The instrument of the Security Council should have been used under Chapter 7 of the Charter which deals with 'Action with respect to threats to the peace, breaches of the peace, and acts of aggression'. The Security Council, under this procedure, should demand from the Government of Pakistan the right to investigate the charges of genocide. It should demand the right to station a military force in East Pakistan to bring acts of violence to an end, and to prevent future acts of violence. It should then demand that a plebiscite should be held in East Pakistan under its auspices to determine the freely expressed wishes of the people of this strife-torn province. Of course the Security Council does not act automatically any more than

Parliament does. In this case I believe that the appropriate action would be a resolution to this effect jointly sponsored by the permanent members of the Security Council. This would create a precedent, but in my view it would be none too early. The precedent of the Security Council imposing a political settlement might then be applied to the Middle East and Cyprus.

In July 1970 I wrote in the *Irish Independent:* 'If nothing more is done by Britain than to reinforce her army presence, I believe that Major Chichester-Clarke's Government will fall to be replaced by a Government led by Mr Faulkner or Mr Craig. By that time any hope of moderation or commonsense will have entirely vanished from the scene.'

I was arguing for a United Nations peacekeeping force and a civilian mediator, and unhappily I feel that my argument has been fully vindicated.

The similarity to Rhodesia but with different actors in the same roles is uncomfortable and uncanny. Instead of Captain O'Neil, you had Mr Garfield Todd. Instead of Major Chichester-Clarke, you had Sir Edgar Whitehead. Mr Brian Faulkner seems destined for the part of Mr Winston Field. Only one further prime ministerial head would then need to roll before Mr Craig, or possibly the Rev. Ian Paisley, performs the act of Mr Ian Smith.

There is one vital difference between Rhodesia in 1965 and Northern Ireland in 1971. British troops are present on the ground.

In my judgment, the Constitution of Northern Ireland should be suspended. The Northern Ireland Government should be dismissed. The Northern Ireland Parliament should be dissolved. A British Cabinet Minister should be appointed Secretary of State for Northern Ireland with full powers. An Executive Governor should be appointed with instructions to set up an advisory council containing representatives of all sections of the community.

The Cabinet and governing party of Northern Ireland is exclusively Protestant. The unique feature of the Province of Northern Ireland is that, unlike anywhere else in the United Kingdom, at least a quarter or possibly a third of the population do not recognize the legitimacy, the impartiality, or authority of the Stormont Government, and malevolent extremists seem bent upon bringing about a complete breakdown in law and order.

Direct rule is now essential since there is no chance of proper co-operation between the UK Government and a more extreme Northern Ireland Government.

Direct rule is, however, the means and not the end. I have long held the view that Britain should ask the United Nations Security Council to set up a peacekeeping force in Northern Ireland similar to that which has been proposed by the United States Government in the Middle East and to that which exists in Cyprus. The reason for Britain referring the matter to the UN is obvious. The present situation constitutes a threat to the peace of the area and involves two sovereign Governments, those of the United Kingdom and the Republic of Ireland.

The operations conducted by the British army in Malaya, East Africa, against EOKA in Cyprus, and now in Northern Ireland itself are not peacekeeping operations at all. They constitute the giving of aid to the civil power. In July 1970, I predicted that the British army would find the task of pacifying Northern Ireland impossible since it was and is, unhappily, regarded by most of the Catholics in Northern Ireland as being the agent of the Stormont Government even though the General Officer Commanding in Northern Ireland has direct access to the British Government.*

Although the British army has much to contribute to peacekeeping operations by way of military and occupational experience, they are novices in the art of peacekeeping as compared with the Canadians and Scandinavians. A British occupying army has as its prerequisite the use of minimum force. A UN peacekeeping force necessarily has to operate under the harsher discipline of not using force unless attacked.

Britain as the sovereign power in Northern Ireland would have an absolute right of choice as to the composition and

*The policy of internment which was adopted in August 1971 has reinforced this impression.

terms of reference of such a force. It is essential that a UN peacekeeping force, if established in Northern Ireland, should be seen by all the people of Northern Ireland as being neutral in the quarrel between Protestants and Catholics. The British Government should bear this important point in mind when the composition of the force is discussed.

A UN peacekeeping force normally carries with it a peacemaking arm. I hope that the British Government would be prepared to ask the Secretary-General U Thant to nominate a civilian mediator of impeccable credentials who could institute talks between Protestant and Catholic leaders in the Province. I do not pretend that these proposals would secure the support of the extremists on either side. It could, however, secure the support of the moderates on both sides whereas the British army at the moment is only acceptable to the moderates on the Protestant side.

Only when physical peace has been restored to the Province through a UN peacekeeping force and a UN mediator can a permanent settlement be contemplated. A variety of possibilities exist. First it might be possible for the Northern Ireland Government to be reconstructed to include a Roman Catholic element as well as Protestants. I cannot regard such a possibility with much hope since during the past fifty years few Catholics have had any reason to accept the intentions of the Stormont Government as being honourable. Although during the past few years the Northern Ireland Government has agreed to a programme of electoral and social reform which, if fully implemented, would give the Catholics of Northern Ireland a proper place in their society, the reforms have come too late and are being implemented too slowly to allow for any optimism about bridge-building between the two religious communities.

It might be necessary for a part of Northern Ireland to be transferred to the Republic. A *condominium* might be set up under which Britain and the Republic of Ireland were the joint sovereign powers and the people of Northern Ireland had dual nationality. It might prove preferable for the Northern Ireland Parliament to be abolished permanently and for the people of Northern Ireland to be more adequately represented at Westminster. There might even have to be a physical transfer of population so that Catholics and Protestants no longer live together in the same State. None of these solutions can even be contemplated while Northern Ireland is in a state of civil commotion.

A peace settlement may take years to achieve. The UN force in Cyprus is now entering its ninth year of existence and a few could doubt that civil war would follow its departure if it were withdrawn now.

The people of Northern Ireland have shown that they cannot govern themselves in peace. An extreme Protestant Government will never be accepted by the large Catholic minority. Three years of reform do not make up for forty-seven years of injustice. If there were to be another General Election Paisleyite candidates would sweep the board as the Rhodesia Front did in 1962.

Britain cannot solve the problem unaided, hence the need for UN troops and a UN mediator like Ambassador Jarring.

I have never pretended that the United Nations could prevent a third world war if a major power bloc is determined to achieve world domination. However, it can, and probably has prevented a major war from starting by accident. I do not believe that the 1914 war could have occurred if the United Nations instrument had existed. It was accidental in the sense that nobody in June 1914 expected war by August. Austria-Hungary delivered an ultimatum to Serbia and then events escalated without anybody being able to control the pace. In 1939 by contrast it was sickeningly plain that if the Democracies did not fight Hitler then, they would have to do so from a weaker position in 1940 or 1941. In 1914 the Security Council would have met and the breathing space provided could have prevented a world war; in 1939 world war was inevitable.

Lord Caradon has often stated that there is nothing wrong with the UN except its members. This is profoundly true. The United Nations is a forum in which Britain can give a lead, but not if our Permanent Representative is instructed to say, as Sir Colin Crowe did last year: 'From now on Britain's interests come first. What is good for Britain is good for the UN.' This is the most arrogantly nationalistic statement that

I have ever heard, though not I fear untypical of the foreign policy of the present Conservative Government. The United Nations will only be an effective instrument when nations put the interests of the international community before their own. I prefer the statement made by Lord Boyle, 'There is a compelling duty on all countries, including our own, to subordinate their national interests to global policies in accordance with the UN Charter.' I look to the next Labour Government to provide this lead.

Chapter 7

Harold Macmillan

'Andrew Devonshire is awfully good with natives. The Devonshires have always been good with natives.' In this whimsical way Harold Macmillan commended to me the appointment in his Government of his nephew by marriage to the post of Minister of State for Commonwealth Relations. We were sitting in the smoking room of the House of Commons, a place much frequented by the then Prime Minister, together with the Carlton Club, particularly when he sensed that his Government was in trouble. He would just come in and sit down next to you and start talking. He never gave any indication that he knew who I actually was. I do not blame him for this. Why, indeed, should anybody spend his declining years in the vexatious task of trying to distinguish one MP from another? He once told me of a visit that he had recently paid to Oxford University of which he had become Chancellor. He had been intrigued at the number of female undergraduates. 'It's all very different now. In my day you had chaps' sisters and cousins in eights week, and then there were gaiety girls.' I sometimes wondered if he mistook me for somebody else, or whether perhaps he was deliberately caricaturing himself to watch my reaction, or whether my profile marked me as a natural member of the Monday Club.

Harold Macmillan's character was indelibly marked by two experiences: the trenches in the First World War and unemployment in his old constituency of Stockton-on-Tees between the wars. There are two other factors which helped to mould his complex character: his near conversion to the Roman Catholic faith by Ronald Knox in his youth, and his near conversion to Socialism in the 1930s. Having myself been converted to both these creeds, I know something of the agony of

I

Above: The Author handing over the presidential chair of the Cambridge Union to his successor, Mr David Price, now MP for Eastleigh and Parliamentary Secretary to the Department of Trade and Industry. (*Illustrated.*) *Right:* The Author when Vice-President of the Cambridge Union with the late Mr Hugh Dalton, at that time Chancellor of the Exchequer. (*London News Agency.*) *Below:* The Author when Chairman of the Coningsby Club with Lord Butler of Saffron Walden, then Chancellor of the Exchequer, and the late Lord Hore-Belisha, formerly Secretary of State for War. (*Van Hallan Press and General Photographic Agency.*)

2
The Author wi
Mzee Jomo Kenyatt
President of Kenya.
(*Kenya Information Services.*)

3
The Author wit
President Kaunda o
Zambia. (*Zambia In-
formation Services.*)

4
The author with the
late Mr Tom Mboya.
(*Kenya Information Ser-
vices.*)

mental uncertainty which in my case left me hovering on the brink for several years before, on each occasion, finally taking the plunge. Macmillan's Christianity was always tinged with Catholicism, and I never felt that he was a genuine Tory at all.

Macmillan's experience of warfare left him with a deep-rooted contempt for those who had not served in the armed forces. I remember his saying at a small dining club of Tory MPs who had entered Parliament in 1959, 'The trouble with Gaitskell is that he has never seen troops under fire.' Butler's lack of military experience doubtless coloured Macmillan's opinion of him. Macmillan's experience of pre-war unemployment made him determined to avoid a confrontation with the trade unions at practically any cost. He was an almost prudish man in matters of sexual morality and this undoubtedly led him to his gullibility in accepting John Profumo's denial of any improper association with Christine Keeler.

I first recall seeing Macmillan in 1948. I was the immediate past Chairman of the Cambridge University Conservative Association and he was the guest speaker at our Annual Dinner. He was then fifty-four but he affected an appearance of exaggerated old age. He spoke of us as the future hope of the Party and of himself as though his career was almost over. In fact it was to last for another fifteen years, and the most triumphant years lay ahead. The following morning I was among those who saw him off at Cambridge station. He wore a cap, a tweed coat and a pipe nestled gently between his lips as he tottered towards the ticket barrier. In fact we were late and the train was on the point of leaving. Seeing this, Macmillan, with the agility of Christopher Chataway, leapt towards the train and caught it as it was moving out of the station.

I did not encounter Macmillan during his period as Minister of Housing, and his record of achievement is well known. I next recall meeting him in February 1955 when he was Defence Minister and the guest of the Coningsby Club of which I was Chairman. I noticed that he drank only ginger ale, and I remember him saying in the course of conversation that a Roman Catholic could never become the Prime Minister of the United Kingdom. This is perhaps of interest in the light of his near conversion. We were dining at the old St Stephens Club in Bridge Street next door to the Houses of Parliament, and at the end of dinner, William Rees-Mogg and I decided to go to the Carlton Club for a drink before we went home. Macmillan offered us a lift in his car and at the last minute said, 'I think that I will come in and join you.' The Club was almost deserted and we spent nearly an hour with Macmillan, who again drank no alcohol. We were perturbed because of rumours which we had heard that Sir Winston Churchill intended to lead the Party into the next election. At this point, a note of steel entered Macmillan's voice and he said that he and some of his colleagues were determined that this should not happen. This led us to believe that an ultimatum had been delivered and would be acted upon.

I did not encounter Macmillan again personally until the end of 1959 when he had already been Prime Minister for nearly three years. He seemed a younger man than when I first saw him eleven years earlier, although he retained his exaggerated manner and shuffling walk. I remember his addressing the new MPs and telling us that the House of Commons was rather like a regiment. He cautioned us against too servile an attitude towards the Whips and referred lightly to his own distinctly rebellious past. He dominated the House at Question Time and whenever he had to deliver a speech. He was a remote figure except for his sudden and somewhat alarming descents on junior back-benchers in the smoking room. He showed how little he troubled to keep in touch with the younger Members of Parliament by the appointment of Knox Cunningham, an elderly and extreme Ulster Unionist as his Parliamentary Private Secretary. I doubt whether he was even familiar with the names of all his Junior Ministers since he left these appointments to the Chief Whip, Martin Redmayne, a rather less capable man than his predecessor, Edward Heath.

It was not clear to me at the end of 1959 that Macmillan had a grand design for his premiership. He had already repaired the Anglo-American alliance, and he had yet to make his 'wind of change' speech and to attempt to secure Britain's entry into the Common Market. It was frequently difficult to recognize the way in which Macmillan's policy was going, if only because of his tendency to do one thing while pretending to do something else. In no sphere was this more evident than in his policy for Britain's evacuation of her African colonies.

Only those who sat in the 1959–64 Parliament will ever know of the traumatic experiences through which the Conservative Party went over events in Africa. For myself the speedy granting of independence to the East African territories of Kenya, Uganda and Tanganyika was most welcome. I had first visited the Federation of Rhodesia and Nyasaland in 1958 and I thought that that partnership was a fraud. Sir Roy Welensky's party was preaching partnership abroad but practising apartheid at home. The younger MPs who were elected in 1959 in many cases shared my views and we were supported by the Colonial Secretary himself, Iain Macleod, and more senior members such as Sir Godfrey Nicholson and Nigel Fisher. Yet we were in a minority in the Party. Stormy meetings of the Party's Colonial Affairs Committee would frequently be held. They were often so full that they were indistinguishable from the 1922 Committee itself.

Macmillan was a genius in disguising from the Right Wing his intention to disengage from Africa as rapidly as possible. I remember overhearing him talking to a group of Conservative back-benchers early in 1960 after he had returned from a visit to the Central African Federation which he was to destroy only three years later: 'It's awfully good of Simon Dalhousie [the Governor-General] to have taken out to Salisbury the vice-regal gold plate which was presented to his ancestor. It's so good for morale.' I particularly noticed how Macmillan would flit from group to group of dejected Conservative MPs in the smoking room administering after-care treatment whenever anything unpleasant had happened such as the release from jail of Dr Banda or Jomo Kenyatta. So-and-so's son had been commissioned in the Coldstream Guards had he, how splendid! X had become Lord Lieutenant of Leicestershire, how well deserved! They say that grouse are plentiful at Swinton this year, admirable. The Conservative MPs would go home to dinner in the comfortable knowledge that their world had not really been disturbed.

This technique was less successful with Sir Roy Welensky

who felt, not without reason, that he had been betrayed by Macmillan when the Monckton Commission considered the question of territories seceding from the Federation despite an assurance that this would not be within its terms of reference. By 1963, however, with Dr Banda in office in Nyasaland and Kenneth Kaunda in office in Northern Rhodesia, Macmillan was able to sink the Federation without protest from Westminster.

Macmillan had less necessity to disguise his European policy. In July 1960, Edward Heath was appointed Lord Privy Seal with a primary responsibility for Europe. A year passed and many ministerial exchanges and meetings took place between British and European ministers before Macmillan was ready to announce on 31 July 1961 the British Government's intention to apply for membership of the European Economic Community. The opposition to this policy in the Conservative Party centred around Sir Derek Walker-Smith, Robin Turton and Sir Ronald Russell; but by far the most effective and vocal opponent of Britain's entry into Europe was a new young MP recently elected at a by-election, Mr Peter Walker. As is known, Britain's entry was vetoed by General de Gaulle in January 1963.

By 1962 Macmillan had begun to age rapidly. It was not appreciated at the time how much of a blow the collapse of the 1960 Paris Summit had been to him. The autumn of 1960 had also seen an acute economic crisis, and early in 1962 the hitherto impregnable seat of Orpington had been lost to the Liberals. A 14,000 majority for the Conservatives had been turned into a minority of nearly 8,000. In July 1962 in an attempt to give a new image to his Government, Macmillan sacked seven ministers in one stroke, a third of his Cabinet. So far from restoring confidence in his leadership this move appeared both to the Parliamentary Party and the public to have been caused by panic. In the autumn of 1962, Macmillan, using the pretext of a report to Martin Redmayne by Peter Tapsell (with whom I was at the time sharing a flat), of a conversation that he had had with a journalist, set up a Tribunal of Inquiry into what was known as the Vassall case. Mr Tom Galbraith, about whom allegations had been made had been completely cleared, although his resignation had previously been accepted. Two journalists had, however, been sent to jail for refusing to reveal their sources of information to the Tribunal. These sentences were deeply resented in Fleet Street, and Macmillan was blamed.

Macmillan had hardly recovered from the heavy blow of de Gaulle's veto when the Profumo scandal broke. I was in Iraq at the time and received a cable from the Chief Whip summoning me back for a vote on a three-line whip on an Opposition vote of censure on the Government's handling of the Profumo affair. I returned with every intention of voting with the Government. However, I listened with growing incredulity to the fact that Macmillan had never seen Profumo about the rumours that had been circulating about his conduct. I remember the querulous tone of the old man's voice when he said, 'I do not move among young people' and the mordant phrase of Nigel Birch 'Never glad confident morning again'. Macmillan seemed on the point of physical collapse but sadly I decided to withhold my vote from him. He had shown a negligence that was inexcusable in a Prime Minister. Twenty-five of my colleagues abstained and several others only supported the Government on the assurance of the Chief Whip that Macmillan would resign by the autumn.

When the autumn came, Macmillan did indeed resign but in circumstances that can hardly have been foreseen by the Whips, and which I have described elsewhere. In October 1963, Sir Alec Douglas-Home became Prime Minister as a result of Macmillan's determination to deny the succession to Rab Butler. First Macmillan wanted Hailsham, then Home. It was he who devised the question that was invariably put to those consulted, 'If there is deadlock between Rab and Quintin, will you accept Alec?' Macmillan must take the blame for the fact that the Conservative Party had a nervous breakdown in public.

Even in his retirement Macmillan showed a certain mockery for the establishment. He rewarded his unpaid private secretary with a peerage; baronetcies went to his press relations officer and his doctor; knighthoods were given to two of his civil service private secretaries and even Lady Dorothy Macmillan's maid was made a member of the Order of the

British Empire. For himself he took nothing. Thus ended the premiership of the most extraordinary Tory Prime Minister of this century. My contemporaries and I used to call him 'The Old Poseur' and there was much of this about him, whether it be the references to his crofter grandfather, his indulging in a certain weakness for the titled aristocracy despite a contempt for newly-created hereditary honours, or his apparent unflappability. In 1971, Macmillan spoke in Bromley saying, 'The curtain has fallen. For an old actor to hang about the green room is a mistake.' The curtain fell in 1963 and I had a seat in the front row of the stalls.

Chapter 8

R. A. Butler

'I'm afraid, my dear Humphry, that we are in for an evening of disaster' was my greeting from R. A. Butler at the dinner party given by Lady Hartwell at the Savoy on the night of the 1970 General Election. It was said with a certain detached relish. Not uncharacteristically Rab went on to make a statement about himself which was almost certainly exaggerated: 'Do you know that during the last two weeks I have received over a thousand letters from people who think that I ought to be Prime Minister.' My mind boggled at the thought of postmen bent double trudging across Trinity Great Court under the weight of this formidable fan mail.

These two sentences summed up certain traits in his character which made Rab, at least for me, a not unattractive character. He was without exception the most egocentric man I have ever met and he drew a certain wry satisfaction from the discomfiture of his colleagues. If this was all that there was to the man he would of course have been a very unattractive person; but superimposed upon his formidable brain, his humane approach to politics, his deliberate encouragement of younger men whom he delighted to help up the rungs of the political ladder, the fact that he was self-centred, jealous of political contemporaries and deliciously indiscreet made him surprisingly lovable.

I first met Rab after the war in Cambridge in the middle 1940s. His father, Sir Montagu Butler, was the Master of my college. It was with Rab's active encouragement that I joined the staff of the Conservative Political Centre, of which he was the Chairman, in 1948. Indeed, it was his reshaping of the Conservative policies which led me to join the Conservative Party at all.

Until the late 1950s, Rab was Chairman of the Conservative

Research Department and of the Conservative Political Centre. For his staff he had chosen people of the ability of Reginald Maudling, Iain Macleod, Enoch Powell, Robin Balniel, Cuthbert Alport, and Peter Tapsell, to name the most conspicuous. The person closest to him was probably the brilliant Peter Goldman whose disaster at Orpington in 1962 wrecked what would undoubtedly have been an outstanding political career. Rab was not afraid of surrounding himself with talented young men. His mind was equal to theirs, and they did not pose a threat to his position in the Party.

The inevitable question which must be asked, even if it cannot be answered wholly satisfactorily, is how it was that Rab, who acted as Deputy Prime Minister to three successive Prime Ministers, never held the supreme post himself. I was not in the House when Eden resigned in January 1957. I was, however, a Party official of medium seniority and therefore possibly saw more of what happened than would have been seen by the general public. It must first be remembered that there was no established process for electing a Conservative Party Leader. What Macmillan later termed the customary processes of consultation did not really exist, if only because entirely different reactions occurred each time a Party Leader died or retired. When Churchill retired, Eden automatically succeeded. I have always believed, and Iain Macleod has confirmed, that when Eden resigned, formal consultation was confined to members of the Cabinet. It is true that Sir Winston Churchill went to the Palace, but this was, I believe, largely a ceremonial visit. Some Members of Parliament and Peers approached their respective Chief Whips, but they were volunteering opinions for which they had not been asked and there is no evidence to show that their gratuitous advice had any influence on the result. The Chairman of the 1962 Committee alone among the back-benchers would have had a right to be consulted and I have no doubt that he was.

Macmillan was chosen by his Cabinet colleagues in preference to Rab, who had been his senior in both the Churchill and Eden Governments, because it was felt that Rab had in some sense been disloyal over the Suez adventure. I knew that Rab had serious misgivings over the mounting of the Suez operation which he has now revealed in his memoirs. Nor when the operation had been launched did he confine these misgivings to his Cabinet colleagues. Nevertheless he felt that if he had resigned, the Government itself would have fallen, and his sense of patriotism told him that this would have been an unforgivable action at a time when British troops were under fire. In fact Butler was designated as acting Prime Minister, in the absence of Eden who was convalescing in Jamaica, during the difficult days leading up to the British withdrawal. Macmillan, by contrast, was, I believe, the most enthusiastic supporter of the Suez action at the beginning and the most ardent advocate of halting half-way through the operation, since as Chancellor of the Exchequer he knew that the American Government would, if necessary, attack the pound. My recollection is that the majority of Party officials, like myself, would have preferred Butler to succeed Eden, but as the Party organization is the property of the Leader, the Central Office very quickly settled down under the increasingly successful premiership of Macmillan.

One tragic happening which took place in 1954 was the death by cancer of Rab's first wife, Sydney. Undoubtedly, this seriously affected his morale in his final months at the Exchequer, and he had not fully recovered from his grief two years later. Although she was not universally popular, Rab adored Sydney who provided a degree both of astringency and backbone in his life. While his marriage to Mollie in 1959 has been extremely happy, and many of Rab's friends have found her an altogether less prickly and more charming woman than Sydney, I believe that had Sydney lived, she would have goaded him to take action to secure that he became Prime Minister in succession to Macmillan in 1963, if not in 1957.

From 1957 until 1963 Rab acted as Deputy Prime Minister. As the linchpin of the Government he carried out a number of major tasks in positions which have been the graveyard of many a political reputation. He was for five years a conspicuously successful Home Secretary. One has only to think of his luckless successor, Henry Brooke, to realize how many land-mines surround this post. As Leader of the House of Commons he was only rivalled by Harry Crookshank in a post in which success eluded men of such ability as Iain Macleod, Richard Crossman and Stafford Cripps. As First Secretary of State and Minister in charge of Central African Affairs, he deftly dissolved the Federation without attracting the accusations of ruthlessness, which were levelled at Iain Macleod, or of dishonesty, which were levelled at Macmillan.

By 1963 it was already clear that Macmillan was past his prime, and his Government had suffered from the twin blows of failure to enter the Common Market and the Profumo scandal. Yet Macmillan persisted in saying publicly that he intended to lead the Party into the next election, when he would already be seventy. It almost seemed as though Macmillan was determined to administer to Butler the treatment which Attlee had given to Herbert Morrison, namely to hang on to the leadership for sufficiently long so as to disqualify him from the succession on the grounds of age.

The situation was suddenly transformed in October 1963 when, as the Conservative Party Annual Conference was about to start, Macmillan was taken to hospital for an operation on his prostate gland. His resignation from the Party leadership was read out to the assembled delegates by Lord Home, who happened to be President of the National Union of Conservative and Unionist Associations for that particular year, and whose single duty would normally have been to preside over the mass rally which always follows the Conference.

There followed the most bizarre Conference in the history of the modern Conservative Party, with considerably more attention being paid to discussions behind the scenes than to debates on the floor. At the end of the Conference four potential leaders had emerged—Butler, Hailsham, Home and Maudling. Back in London, the Lord Chancellor was given the task of polling the Cabinet; the Chief Whips in the Commons and the Lords looked after the MPs and Peers; and Lords Poole and Chelmer and Dame Peggy Shepherd were responsible for interpreting the view of the prospective candidates and the voluntary workers in the constituencies. Nothing like this had ever happened before – and the absence of openly-competing candidates and the fact that the pollsters were also the tellers, who actually interpreted and even weighted, on some unknown formula, the figures which were never disclosed – ensured that it would never happen again.

The king-makers on this occasion included the Chief Whip, Mr Martin Redmayne, and the Chairman of the 1922 Committee, then Major John Morrison. A friend of mine spent the weekend after the Party Conference had ended and before the consultations had formally begun at Major Morrison's country house. The Chief Whip was a fellow guest. My friend subsequently reported to me that Mr Redmayne and Major Morrison in conversations which he witnessed were already taking it for granted that Lord Home would be the successor.

I had little doubt that Hailsham had the support of the constituency workers, and I believe that Rab had a clear majority among Members of Parliament. However a second a vital question was put to most of those consulted, namely, 'If there is deadlock between Rab and Quintin, would you accept Alec Home?' In this way Macmillan got the answer that he wanted (he had earlier abandoned Hailsham for Home) and it was on this basis that he advised the Queen to send for Lord Home.

I remember standing outside Buckingham Palace and witnessing the arrival of Lord Home; from there I went to the Carlton Club for lunch with William Rees-Mogg and Peter Goldman. Rab was having lunch upstairs in the ladies' annexe with Mollie and James Ramsden, his former Parliamentary Private Secretary. We joined them for coffee and the three of us urged Rab to refuse to serve in a Home administration. We knew that Macleod and Powell had already refused and we believed that if Rab stood firm, Maudling and Boyle would also refuse to serve. Home would then have to inform the Queen that he could not form a Government. Rab appeared to accept our advice and while we waited at the Carlton Club, Sir Michael Fraser, the Director of the Conservative Research Department, telephoned Peter Goldman to inform us that Rab had seen Home and had refused to serve in his Government. I appeared on three television programmes that evening and not only deplored the choice of Home but strongly criticized the method of choosing. The following morning, after seeing Home for the third time, Rab agreed to become Foreign Secretary.

Our general had surrendered and only Iain Macleod and Enoch Powell refused office under Home.

I have discussed these events since with Rab and the reason that he always gave for the action which he took was that he believed that any other course would have split the Party. I have always disagreed with this view. I believe that had Rab acted as we advised, not only would he have become Prime Minister but the Conservative Party would have won the General Election of 1964.

After Lord Home – Sir Alcc Douglas-Home as he was to become – succeeded to the premiership, it was clear that Rab had lost his appetite for politics. He was Foreign Secretary for barely a year and I only remember his making two or three speeches in the Commons. During the 1964 General Election he made some typically indiscreet remarks to George Gale in a railway carriage. He predicted that the tide was turning against the Conservatives and when it was suggested that the Prime Minister had a high regard for Edward Heath, he replied, 'I always thought Alec was rather bored by him, as a man I mean, not as a Minister'. Early in 1965 Rab gratefully accepted the Mastership of Trinity College, Cambridge, and a life peerage at the hands of Harold Wilson, the new Prime Minister.

I shall always remember Rab as the author of many celebrated phrases: 'The best Prime Minister we have' was his ambiguous description of Eden in 1956. 'I speak to you as Her Majesty's Principal Secretary of State' was his Curzonesque introduction to a speech delivered to the Conservative Party Conference in 1962. I was once flabbergasted when Rab turned to me at a Coningsby Club dinner which I was chairing and said, 'If it wasn't for what I did during the war, none of us would be sitting round this table tonight'. I recalled that he had spent almost the entire war as Education Minister, an important domestic post but hardly a sphere in which battles were won. I was amazed when he told me, in another moment of indiscretion, that he had seen, when Home Secretary, a police report on the then illegal sexual activities of one of his Cabinet colleagues.

He will be remembered by the public as the author of the 1944

Education Act which bears his name and as the most successful of the post-war Chancellors of the Exchequer.

Many people have accused Rab of disloyalty. This was true in that he could not resist recounting anecdotes about his colleagues, usually to their disadvantage. Yet he kept faith with his Party, even to the extent of fearing to split it over the leadership question in 1963. As the person in charge of policy from 1945 until 1964, he gave Conservatism a humane face. It is not without significance that his departure from politics was followed within a few years by that of Sir Edward Boyle. The death of Iain Macleod was a tragedy from which the Party has yet to recover. I joined the Party of Butler, Macleod and Boyle in 1947. When they departed there was no place for me within its folds.

Chapter 9

Iain Macleod

I first met Iain Macleod in 1948 when he was in charge of Home Affairs at the Conservative Research Department and I had just left Cambridge and joined the Staff of the Conservative Political Centre. He was a senior colleague who was obviously destined to go places. We did not know each other very well.

I came to know him better in 1951 when he was Director of the London Municipal Society (the Tory organization for London Local Government) in addition to being Member for Enfield. I was Political Education Officer for the Conservative Party in the London area and we jointly ran week-end conferences for LCC candidates. At one of the sessions, Iain himself took the part of a Labour Councillor and the candidates had to answer a speech which he made, and try to floor him during the question period. Iain's performance as a Labour Councillor was so convincing that some of the candidates were actually red-faced with rage at the arguments which he put forward. I had no idea until then of his acting ability.

Another occasion which I recall, again in 1951, was a dinner of the Coningsby Club at which Iain was the guest speaker. The only people present were the Chairman, a deaf and drunken old Conservative Peer and myself. The Chairman had forgotten to send out the notices. Iain was not unnaturally furious and refused to speak again to the Coningsby Club. I finally persuaded him to do so in 1955 at our Annual Dinner on the 150th anniversary of Disraeli's birth. He spoke movingly and brilliantly.

I cannot claim to have known Iain at all well until my election to Parliament in 1959. I found myself in complete agreement with his Colonial policy, starting as it did with the 1960 Kenya Constitutional Conference. During this period I saw Iain reasonably frequently, and invariably had a private meeting with him on my return from visits to Africa—which took place three or four times a year.

In the spring of 1961, it was clear that Iain was in serious trouble with the Tory Party Right Wing and he appeared to be deriving his support almost entirely from the 1959 entry to Parliament. I persuaded him to ask about thirty Members of Parliament for a drink at his flat. He left the question of invitations to Charles Longbottom and me, but I recall people like Sir Peter Agnew, Sir John Vaughan Morgan, and Sir Tufton Beamish, among others, being present. Iain felt that this drinks party did a great deal to restore his position among the more senior members of the 1922 Committee.

In was in the month of June 1961 that Iain published his proposals for the Constitution of Northern Rhodesia. These proposals seemed to go back on an announcement that he had made the previous February. Iain was adamant that Kaunda's party could win. I remember his going through the mathematics with me in his office in the old Colonial Office at Church House, Westminster. For once Iain was wrong; his successor, Reginald Maudling, with the threat of his own resignation, obtained a small but decisive shift in favour of the Africans, and even so a Coalition Government had to be formed between Kaunda and Nkumbula on a wafer-thin majority over Welensky's territorial party (the UFP). I do not know to this day whether Iain deluded himself that his figures were right (which they manifestly were not), or whether after Kenya and Nyasaland and an intitial row over Northern Rhodesia he shirked another fight with the Tory Right. On the whole I believe the former to be true. I do not rule out the latter because, although Iain was a politician of exceptional courage, there is a limit to what most people can take.

During his period as Chairman of the Party from 1961 to 1963, we had fewer official meetings with each other, but we met reasonably frequently, either over a drink in the smoking room or over lunch or dinner.

Iain's refusal to serve under Sir Alec Douglas-Home in October 1963 coincided with my own disgust at the so-called customary processes of consultation. I did not disguise from

Iain that I had made clear to the Whips that my sole choice for the leadership was R. A. Butler. I felt Rab deserved it on seniority and merit and I hoped that when Rab gave up, Iain would become his natural successor. Iain told me that he thought that my attitude was entirely right. He did not rate his chances of becoming Leader in 1963 at all high, but he thought there was an outside chance, which I frankly did not.

I was in Switzerland in January 1964 staying with Christopher Chataway on a skiing holiday when I read Iain's 4,000-word article in the *Spectator* on how the leadership contest had been rigged. I returned to London two days later and the following week asked Iain to lunch with me at the White Tower Restaurant. I found him in the depths of despair. The reaction to his article had been ferociously hostile and he talked to me about giving up politics altogether and concentrating on writing. I told him that this was quite unreasonable and that if he left politics, he would betray a large number of young members who saw him as the only leader who could preserve the radical future of the Party. Iain told me that he was keeping away from the House of Commons since he could not bear to go there any more. I subsequently persuaded him to go into the smoking room with me to have a drink one evening, pointing out that sooner or later he would have to go there. We were ostentatiously cut by every Tory in the room.

When the 1964 General Election came, I invited Iain to be the only outside speaker in my campaign in Lancaster. Several of my constituency officers said that they would boycott the meeting. I told them that as the candidate, I was entirely free to choose my supporting speakers and that was the end of the matter. Iain was in magnificent form and received a standing ovation at the end.

After the 1964 election, I went on a visit to East Africa which included the independence celebrations in Zambia. I was, therefore, away when the Shadow Cabinet appointments were announced. Iain told me that he had chosen the position of Opposition Spokesman on Steel since he thought (wrongly as he later admitted) that this would be in the forefront of parliamentary controversy and his magnificent debating power would be fully utilized in the House. As things turned out,

he Author with Archbishop
lakarios, President of Cyprus.

'he Author with U Thant,
ugust, 1967.

7
The Author with Mr Harol
Wilson. (*Michael Arron.*)

8
From left to right: The Rt Hon. Edward Heath, MP, the Author, the late Sir David Owen, Administrator of the UN Development Programme, The Rt Hon. Harold Wilson, MP, then Prime Minister, and The Rt Hon. Jeremy Thorpe, MP, Leader of the Liberal Party, April, 1968. (*The Associated Press Ltd.*)

Wilson did not attempt to nationalize the steel industry on a majority of five (later to be reduced to three), and Iain only made two speeches as Opposition Steel Spokesman between October 1964 and July 1965, both of which were effective.

Shortly after the 1964 election, I told Iain that I thought that a serious attempt must be made to restore him to a central position in the Party. I offered him the services of a full-time personal assistant, Mr David Rogers, who was paid for by the merchant bank of which I was a director—Sumption Berkeley. I also gathered around him a small group of MPs who would meet from time to time to plan the strategy for his return. At no time did we contemplate the overthrow of Alec Douglas-Home by Iain, but we worked to ensure that if and when Sir Alec went (and we hoped that his departure would be later rather than earlier), Iain would be in a strong position to gain the succession.

In February 1965, Sir Alec announced a new method for electing the Party Leader, and in May and June 1965, it became clear that the Heath lobby was on the move. Iain had to endure an enforced silence as a front-bencher. Heath, as Shadow Chancellor, had put up a good performance in fighting the 1965 Finance Bill. I was actually on my way back from the Seychelles when Sir Alec announced his resignation as the Party Leader on Thursday, 22 July 1965. I received by hand a handwritten letter from Iain on my return the following day which read:

> *My dear Humphry,*
> I'm so sorry you weren't with us when the decisive moment arrived yesterday: I wanted to talk to you very much. But I'm sure I did the right thing and I think you agree. So there it is. And most particularly I want to thank you for so much help and loyalty and friendship. I am very grateful indeed.
> See you soon.
>
> *Ever,*
> IAIN

In fact I did not agree that it was right for Iain to withdraw from the contest and I told him so, but since he had already announced in public that he would in no circumstances be a candidate, it was too late. I did not think that Iain would win. A careful calculation made by us indicated that he might get about forty votes. However, I wanted him to stand if only to establish a future claim. Iain became Chancellor in Heath's Shadow Cabinet.

In the ballot for private members bills in the 1965–6 session, I came second and decided to introduce the Sexual Offences Bill making homosexual acts between consenting male adults in private no longer a criminal offence. When this Bill was given a second reading on 11 February 1966, Iain cancelled an engagement which he had outside London in order to be present and vote in support. (Incidentally, Iain had voted in favour of Sidney Silverman's Bill to abolish capital punishment at the end of 1964. Ted Heath had abstained and Reginald Maudling voted in favour of the retention of hanging.)

My main point of difference with Iain at the end of 1965 and in the early months of 1966 was his opposition to sanctions against Rhodesia. Many people at the time had thought that Iain was currying favour with the right wing. I never believed that this was the case. Iain always maintained that sanctions as conceived by the British Government at that time would not work and he has proved to be right. He also said to me several times that he believed that he could have found a negotiated settlement to the Rhodesian problem. I do not believe that he was right in this view, nor do I think that Iain ever grasped the essential difference between Rhodesia and other African colonies, namely the existence of many more Europeans and the lack of British troops on the ground.

The fact that our difference of view in no way altered our relationship is shown by the following letter which Iain wrote to me on 15 March 1966 in the middle of the election:

> *My dear Humph,*
> This written before I sleep—in a sleeper going south from Preston. Just to say that there is no one whose success in this goddamn election means more to me than does yours. If there is any message I can send you – I'm quite respectable now! – just tell me. My phone number is Potters Bar

52381. But I'm home really only on Sundays while the circus is on.

Ever,
IAIN

This was a completely spontaneous letter and I was very touched to receive it. I asked Iain if he would write a letter for publication in the *Lancaster Guardian* (as Alec Douglas-Home also did) saying that no Conservative should abstain from voting for me because of my Bill. At least a thousand did abstain and I believe that the Bill was probably responsible for the loss of my seat.

On the day after polling day when my defeat was already known, Iain telephoned me in my cottage near Lancaster and asked when I was returning to London. I told him that I would be coming back the following Monday and he came to my London flat to spend an hour or so with me talking about my future. Inevitably, from then on I saw him somewhat less frequently since I was no longer a Member of Parliament, but we regularly lunched or dined together about once a month.

Iain and I were at one with each other on the East African Asian Bill which he opposed. He regarded this measure as a betrayal of promises given by successive Colonial Secretaries of which he was one. We did not see eye to eye on the Race Relations Bill of 1968 which he thought wholly unnecessary, and I resigned from the Conservative Party on 18 April 1968 when the Conservative Party decided to oppose the Bill. My resignation received considerable publicity since Heath wrote me a reply of over a thousand words in length (see pp. 38–40). Iain rang me up and asked why I had not consulted him, and I told him that I knew that he would have cautioned me not to resign, that my mind was already made up and that a talk with him would only have made matters more difficult. He was friendly and sympathetic and did not utter a word of reproach.

On Monday, 22 April 1968 Iain wrote a letter to *The Times* which started, 'I can at least agree with you that the departure of Mr Humphry Berkeley is a real loss to the Conservative Party. I believe he will return.' I regarded this as an act of great generosity on the part of the Shadow Chancellor to an unpopular figure who had just left the Party.

In September 1968, Iain was the Conservative speaker at the Annual Dinner of the United Nations Association held at the Guildhall. He paid public tribute to my qualities of leadership as Chairman of the United Nations Association and expressed the hope that I would return to the Conservative Party.

In 1969 after the Conservative Party had announced that they would work the Race Relations Act, I had a number of lunches with Iain who sought to persuade me to return to the Party—which I did in September 1969. Iain immediately issued a public statement welcoming my return. It is quite clear to me now that I should never have rejoined the Conservative Party. I felt uneasy when Sir Edward Boyle, who asked me to dinner on 18 September 1969 to celebrate my return to the Party, told me that he did not intend to serve in a Conservative Cabinet after the election in the event of a Conservative victory. He accepted the post of Vice-Chancellor of Leeds University shortly afterwards.

My last telephone conversation with Iain was in May 1970 after I had written an article in the *Guardian* saying that I intended to vote Labour at the forthcoming election—because of the Conservative Party's intention to sell arms to South Africa, its support of the South African cricket tour, and its commitment to a further round of talks with the Smith regime. Iain spoke to me more in sorrow than in anger. Both of us realized that my break with the Conservative Party was inevitable and irrevocable. We each said that our personal friendship would not be altered but to my sorrow this was the last time we ever spoke to each other.

The description of Iain by Lord Salisbury as 'too clever by half' was to dog him for his last ten years. As a statement of fact, whether cleverness meant intellect or, as most thought, deviousness, it was untrue. Iain had a good quick mind and great strength of character, but in no sense could he have been termed an intellectual. He was not widely read, even though he surprised me once by saying that he reread each of the novels of C. P. Snow once a year. He had no taste for pictures, or furniture. His pastimes verged on vulgarity—gambling at

Crockfords or Whites, going to the Derby, watching football matches. He had little conversation outside politics although he had the capacity to make politics a romance. In my experience he was utterly straightforward. Had he been more sibylline, he would not have antagonized the Conservative Right Wing when he was Colonial Secretary. He was not a successful Leader of the House of Commons because he was naturally pugnacious. He was never to escape from the charge of disloyalty for having refused office in the Government of Sir Alec Douglas-Home and subsequently revealing all that he knew about the strange process by which Sir Alec had become Prime Minister. He was not a good-looking or even a charming man, yet he had so strong a hold over the hearts and the imagination of the young that he possessed a greater political magnetism than any of his contemporaries.

Chapter 10

Edward Heath

It is a bizarre biological fact that the Conservative Party can only be directed along a sensible left-wing path by a Leader with impeccable aristocratic connections. What is permitted to the fourteenth earl or the consort of a duke's daughter cannot be attempted by the grammar-school boy from Broadstairs who, to prove his genuine conservatism, has wrenched the Conservative Party so far to the right that it is no longer recognizable to me as the Party which I represented in Parliament only six years ago.

This is as much a criticism of the Conservative Party as it is of Mr Heath. The Conservative Party under Mr Heath has become divisive, sectional, arrogant and insensitive. The support within the Party for Mr Heath's display of ill manners towards his fellow Prime Ministers at the Singapore Conference is only one example of this fact.

I was introduced to Edward Heath by William Deedes at the Conservative Party Conference at Llandudno in 1948. Heath was prospective parliamentary candidate for Bexley; I had just joined the staff of the Conservative Political Centre. Deedes, who was prospective parliamentary candidate for Ashford, told me how he had defeated Heath for the nomination in that constituency. He had appeared in front of the Selection Committee in a tweed jacket; Heath had worn a city suit.

Heath made no impression on me, either favourable or unfavourable. I remember his winning Bexley in February 1950, but only on account of the extreme narrowness of his majority—133. When he was made a Junior Whip a year later, I was not surprised—he seemed good Whip material.

Throughout Heath's eight-year period in the Whips Office, I did not know him well. I met him from time to time as a

Party official, sometimes socially in the Carlton Club, and we exchanged Christmas cards each year.

An incident occurred in 1956 which made me aware of a degree of intolerance in his character. I was lunching at the Carlton Club with a friend who is now a Conservative Member of Parliament. Heath came into the dining-room alone, and as is customary in the club, asked if he might join us. My friend and I – convinced abolitionists – were discussing capital punishment. The Government which Heath was serving as Chief Whip had run into some trouble. Sidney Silverman's Bill had a majority in the House of Commons because the Conservative and Labour abolitionists had joined forces. There was no such majority in the House of Lords. The Government was, therefore, forcing through Parliament a compromise measure which retained the death penalty for four categories of murder. Heath tried to convince us that the compromise was sensible, whereas we were adamant that it would not work. Heath became abusive; he called us soft and then relapsed into a sullen silence, refusing to join us for coffee afterwards. Neither of us was in Parliament, but we were both prospective Conservative candidates, and we were shocked at this display of anger and rudeness on the part of the Government Chief Whip.

When I entered the House of Commons, Heath had ceased to be Chief Whip and had become Minister of Labour. His performances at the Dispatch Box were somewhat clumsy, but I put this down to eight years of enforced silence in the Whips Office. Heath made little public impact as Minister of Labour, indeed he only held the post for nine months. It is difficult in the light of the Industrial Relations legislation of 1971 to believe that either he or the trade union leaders would have found each other congenial.

In the summer of 1960 Heath moved to the Foreign Office with full Cabinet rank as Lord Privy Seal with primary responsibility for European Affairs. I recall him reporting at length to the House on the Common Market negotiations; reports that were solid and painstaking, but also rather pedestrian and dull. I can believe that his mastery of detail in the conducting of the negotiations was prodigious. I have been told this many times by senior civil servants. At this time I was a member of the British delegation to the Council of Europe and met Heath, both officially and socially, at Strasbourg. I became aware of his cold exterior, and of seeing ripples of unease spread among those surrounding him at receptions and meals. I do not recall Heath playing any part in the events surrounding the resignation of Harold Macmillan and the emergence of Sir Alec Douglas-Home, nor, interestingly enough, was his name even mentioned for the post of Leader which he was to gain through a secret ballot of Members of Parliament less than two years later.

In Sir Alec's Government, Heath went to the Board of Trade with the resounding title of Secretary of State for Industry, Trade and Regional Development and President of the Board of Trade. He was responsible for the abolition of Resale Price Maintenance; in this I supported him. He made many enemies among the members of the Conservative Parliamentary Trade and Industry Committee, as much because of his manner as their hostility towards his measure. At the time I was impressed with his determination to push through legislation which was necessary but unpopular.

I had strongly opposed the process by which Sir Alec had become Party Leader. In January 1964, when he was still Prime Minister, Sir Alec had promised me that after the General Election this process would be reviewed. In February 1965 Sir Alec announced a new procedure for electing the Party Leader by the secret ballot of members of the Parliamentary Party. This system was almost identical to that outlined in a memorandum which I had sent to him the previous December.

In the early part of 1965, I was a member of a group which used to meet fairly frequently with Iain Macleod. However, we were in no sense plotting for Iain Macleod to overthrow Sir Alec. Iain had incurred considerable unpopularity for refusing to serve in Sir Alec's Cabinet, and all of us were concerned to restore his reputation in the Party as an unrivalled parliamentarian and political fighter. Naturally the adequacy of the Party leadership was from time to time discussed, and Iain always firmly maintained that no man of honour could seek to replace Sir Alec and yet remain in his Shadow Cabinet.

Heath had become Shadow Chancellor in the Shadow Cabinet that Sir Alec Douglas-Home had formed in 1964. More important, he had also replaced Rab Butler as Chairman of the Conservative Research Department and Policy Chief. In this capacity Heath gained firm control of the policy-making machinery of the Party. In 1965 he invited me to sit on a Committee chaired by Sir Edward Boyle on the machinery of government. Members included such distinguished former civil servants as Sir Edward Fellowes, former Clerk of the House of Commons, and Sir Timothy Bligh, former Principal Private Secretary to Mr Macmillan and to Sir Alec Douglas-Home. We sat for nearly two years, and the changes in ministerial structure which Heath introduced into his Cabinet in the autumn of 1970 were almost identical to our recommendations; moreover, those to do with external affairs were actually written by me.

In May 1965, it became clear that a pro-Heath lobby was being mounted with the objective of replacing Sir Alec as Party Leader at the earliest opportunity. A number of Heath's henchmen, including a member of the present Cabinet, privately suggested to their parliamentary colleagues that they should write to Mr Whitelaw, the Chief Whip, or Mr du Cann, the Party Chairman, expressing their misgivings over the leadership which Sir Alec was providing. I have always believed that an article by Mr William Rees-Mogg in the *Sunday Times* of July 1965 finally decided Sir Alec to resign, but his confidence must have been seriously eroded by the activities of Mr Heath's supporters during the two preceding months.

Thanks to their careful planning, Heath's team had located almost every Heath supporter before Sir Alec's resignation had been announced. It was in this untypical way that the Party which places a special premium on personal loyalty elected its first leader to be chosen by a recognizably democratic method.

It is ironical that at any moment between 1966 and 1970, when Heath's personal popularity always trailed well behind that of his Party, Sir Alec, by a gesture, could have removed Heath from the leadership. He was too much of a gentleman to perform such an act.

As Opposition Leader, Heath had little chance to display

his liking of power. He did, however, show petulance and a refusal to have near him people of independence and ability. He also had a tendency to interfere in matters of detail which would not normally have concerned a Party Leader. In the summer of 1966 I had delivered a series of Third Programme broadcasts entitled 'Government by Consent'. I was approached by the Conservative Political Centre and asked if they could be published by them in pamphlet form. The copyright belonged to the BBC but the necessary permission was sought and obtained. When the pamphlet was in page proof form, I was asked by Sir Michael Fraser, the Deputy Chairman of the Conservative Party, to have a drink with him. Clearly greatly embarrassed, Fraser informed me that Heath had vetoed the publication because one of the broadcasts dealing with the Commonwealth, and African independence in particular, had been thought to be too radical. The pamphlet was immediately published by the Bow Group.

This was the first indication that I had that Heath took a decidedly more right-wing position on African matters even than Sir Alec Douglas-Home. In 1966 I stayed with Kenneth Kaunda in the State House, Lusaka, at the time of the Commonwealth Conference. Kaunda had sent Kapwepwe, his Foreign Minister, to London to represent him instead of attending personally, as a protest at the Labour Government's handling of the Rhodesian problem. On my return, I naturally reported on my conversations with Kaunda to the Prime Minister and also to Heath who seemed to be totally uninterested in the affairs of the African continent. I remember in particular his saying, 'Mike Pearson says that the Conference is a complete waste of time'. Subsequently I obtained invitations for Mr Heath from three African Presidents asking him to visit their countries. I delivered these personally; Heath was reserved and unwilling to commit himself. Had he visited independent Africa at any time between 1966 and 1969, I do not believe that he would have involved himself and this country in the disastrous pledge to sell arms to South Africa. I went through even greater misgivings about Heath in 1969 when a friend of mine, an academic who works closely with the British mission at the United Nations, told me of a conversation that he had

had with Heath. My friend had praised the work of Lord Caradon. 'He is a traitor to his country' was Heath's response. Startled, my friend asked for elucidation but Heath merely repeated the charge without explanation. It is this reaction to Commonwealth events – the reaction of an ignorant suburban housewife – that led Heath into a position of complete isolation at the Singapore Conference.

His removal of Edward du Cann from the Conservative Party chairmanship and his replacement of him by Anthony Barber was the act of a jealous unsure man. Since almost all the recent reforms at the Conservative Central Office leading to victory in 1970 had been carried out by Edward du Cann, it was distinctly ungenerous of Heath to give du Cann twenty-four hours' notice to quit, only a few weeks before the annual party conference. His exclusion of Edward du Cann from his Cabinet constitutes a broken pledge, since when he resigned as Chairman of the Party, du Cann was promised a post in the next Conservative Cabinet. His dismissal of Enoch Powell from the Shadow Cabinet, often portrayed as a courageous act, was the result of a virtually unanimous call from his colleagues in the Shadow Cabinet to do so. Heath was decidedly less brave in rebutting Powellism; indeed his speeches on race and immigration have grown progressively less liberal since Powell's notorious speech of April 1968.

Many people have expressed surprise at the Prime Minister's conduct during the period that he has been in office. I suggest that his behaviour was predictable. For many years he has subordinated his emotions to the acquisition of power. He is the first Prime Minister to have been the Chief Whip in a previous Government, an experience which stood him in good stead when his supporters were undermining the position of Sir Alec Douglas-Home. The qualities which are the essential tools of a Chief Whip's trade are less successful when deployed at a Commonwealth Conference. If the Commonwealth breaks up through Britain's action, this country will become a smaller, narrower and nastier place, just as Mr Heath has made the Conservative Party a smaller and narrower party.

Mention must of course be made of the Prime Minister's commitment to Europe which has been the principal public hallmark of his political career. It is a commitment that I share with him; that indeed is why I sought and obtained appointment by Harold Macmillan to the British parliamentary delegation to the Council of Europe and to the Council of the Western European Union. Heath became Prime Minister at a uniquely favourable time for someone holding views on Europe as strongly as he does. He should not be grudged this piece of chronological good fortune. In the future he will no doubt go through periods of dark despair as most of his predecessors have done. It should, however, be noted that by June 1970 when Heath became Prime Minister the awesome figure of de Gaulle had vanished from the French political scene. A year later when the Common Market negotiations were well under way de Gaulle's successor, President Pompidou, had a positive reason for wanting Britain in the Community. Germany had floated the mark, she was clearly the dominant power in the Common Market, and also Britain was needed by France as an ally. For Britain this meant a redefining in the twentieth century of her historic European role in previous centuries—the provision of the balance of power.

I do not doubt that Heath has obtained terms for Britain's entry into the Community which are as favourable as Harold Wilson could have obtained three years earlier, although it must be added that Heath, for reasons already stated, was much more favourably placed. That Heath is a tough and determined negotiator has been proved beyond doubt. There remain however his substantial character defects which I have described in considerable, albeit subjective detail. He appears to have no power of communication. He treats his most loyal colleagues with a curmudgeonliness which I would be reluctant to believe had I not been told of this by so many first-hand witnesses. He treats the House of Commons and his own senior back-benchers with an arrogance which is deeply resented. The British public is becoming aware of this and it does not like what it sees and hears. Mr Heath should remember that Churchill, in the darkest days of the war when he held almost unbridled power, was deeply sensitive to public opinion, and that even so, his public, so faithfully served by him in times of danger, turned on him when the moment of danger was over.

I doubt whether a simple analysis can be made of any dramatic swing of the political pendulum. I sense, however, that in 1945 one among many complex motives which impelled the electorate to reject Churchill can be picked out. The British people dislike unbridled power. We have no carefully written constitutional checks and balances. Perhaps the British public felt that it had to administer a rebuff to Churchill in 1945 to preserve our traditional freedoms. Certainly the General Election result in 1970 showed that the British electorate does not necessarily behave predictably.

I have no doubt that Britain should enter Europe. I question whether Heath has the personal qualities and judgment to lead the British people along the path which he wishes them to follow, and even if he is successful in this, whether he can survive. Heath has, I believe, greater powers of self-destruction than any Prime Minister within living memory. His incapacity to show gratitude for services rendered is building up a stockpile of throbbing resentment. I would view his downfall without pity but without relish. It takes a malevolent man to revel in the destruction of the political career of another, particularly if, even though only on the fringes of power, he has suffered political reverses as I have done. My harshest critic has never called me malevolent.

I feel instinctively that Heath's career will end, as did that of Lloyd George, in political ruin, although for different reasons. He may even damage his Party for many years to come. His behaviour towards his Commonwealth colleagues may destroy the Commonwealth itself. This I could not forgive. If however despite my doubts he leads Britain into Europe, I will not withhold my praise.

Chapter 11

Harold Wilson

I first spoke to Harold Wilson when he was Leader of the Opposition in 1964. I was, although a Conservative Member of Parliament, a member of a UNA delegation which he received in the summer of 1964 to discuss the attitude that a Labour Government would adopt toward the UN. In answer to a question from me Mr Wilson said that his Government would appoint a Minister as Britain's Permanent Representative to the UN, and that the person would be of considerable international standing. I immediately thought of Sir Hugh Foot and my guess proved to be right.

I first had dealings with Harold Wilson after he became Prime Minister. Through a mutual friend, Sir Geoffrey Gibbs had asked me to go to see him in February 1965. Sir Geoffrey told me that his brother Sir Humphrey Gibbs the Governor of Rhodesia had discovered that his telephone at Government House in Salisbury was being tapped, and his mail was being intercepted. This was nearly a year before UDI. Using the services of a guest who had been staying at Government House Sir Humphrey had smuggled a letter out of Rhodesia to his brother telling him this, and also saying that he had no instructions on what he should do in the event of UDI taking place. I wrote a personal letter to the Prime Minister at the request of Sir Geoffrey Gibbs explaining the predicament. The Prime Minister replied to my letter personally, saying that instructions as to what Sir Humphrey should do in the event of UDI would be taken out to him by the Lord Chancellor and Arthur Bottomley (the Commonwealth Secretary) who were due to visit Rhodesia shortly, and would be staying at Government House. It so happens that I travelled to Rhodesia on the same plane as the Government party. Arthur Bottomley sat next to me for part of the journey and confirmed that the instructions were with him.

I continued to take a close interest in the Rhodesian scene throughout 1965. I had been in Zambia during the independence celebrations in October 1964. At this time General Anderson who commanded the Rhodesian Army was dismissed by Ian Smith. While I was attending a garden party on 24 October 1964 given by Sir Evelyn Hone – whose governorship of Northern Rhodesia was to cease – rumours spread that the independence of Southern Rhodesia would illegally be declared that very night. This did not in the event happen but from my contacts in Rhodesia I became increasingly sure that the Smith Government would take illegal action before long. I was dismayed when first Arthur Bottomley and later the Prime Minister stated in advance of UDI, that if this were to happen Britain would in no circumstances use force. I regarded this assurance as being the green light to Ian Smith and his colleagues to go ahead.

I can understand why Harold Wilson ruled out the use of force after the event. His parliamentary majority at the time was three. Many members of the Conservative Party in Parliament and possibly a majority of Conservatives in the country wanted Smith to win. It was as much as some forty colleagues and I could do to get the Conservative leadership to accept sanctions at all. If Wilson had used force and failed, the full fury of the Conservative Party and popular feeling might have pulled him down. The essence of the operation would have to have been speedy success.

I in fact believed that force should have been used on 11 November. I also believe that if this had happened the rebellion would have been over in forty-eight hours. I would have dropped paratroopers to capture Government House and release the beleaguered Governor, and would have asked him to broadcast to the people of Rhodesia telling them to be loyal to him as the representative of the Queen. I wanted in fact to say this during my speech in the House of Commons on 12 November 1965 – the day after UDI – but I was persuaded by some of my friends that this would totally discredit those of us in the Conservative Party who wanted to topple Smith, and that there would be a ferocious reaction from the Right Wing of the Party which would force the leadership to come out against sanctions.

I was persuaded to refrain from advocating the use of force against my better judgment and I am not satisfied that the advice that I was given was right, although I accepted it at the time. If, however, an ordinary back-bencher like myself could be persuaded that he could make a speech which would force the Leader of the Conservative Party to oppose sanctions it is even more understandable that the Prime Minister of a Labour Government resting on a majority of three should hesitate to clash head on with the Opposition. While I remain astonished that so intelligent a man as Harold Wilson should have broken the rules of good poker playing by ruling out military intervention in advance, I can confirm that he received very little help from Mr Heath when UDI occurred. Throughout the first four weeks, which could have been decisive had sanctions been applied at once, Heath wobbled, looked over his shoulder and tried to gain Party points. He sent his Parliamentary Private Secretary to see me to find out what sanctions I advocated. James Prior seemed astonished when I replied 'Anything which will bring down Smith'. The lack of Mr Heath's leadership was apparent when the House of Commons was asked to vote on a Government motion on oil sanctions. We were told to abstain. A group of us numbering about forty decided to vote with the Government, a similar number voted against, and so the Conservative Party split three ways. We had a meeting with the Chief Whip Mr Whitelaw beforehand and he seemed on the edge of a nervous breakdown. At one point he had a physical spasm of shivering and trembling which brought him close to physical collapse. No Party Leader should allow his Chief Whip to get into this state through indecision at the top.

I had two private meetings with Harold Wilson in the first month after UDI. At the first I gave him as clear an analysis of the Rhodesian scene as I could. I was able to describe in some detail each member of Smith's rebellious government. I found that he had already formed a pretty shrewd judgment of those whom he had met, except for Ian Smith, whom he still believed to be a moderate in bad company. I had known Smith for eight years and formed a different view. I also talked to the Prime Minister about moderate Europeans who might be included in a Government after UDI had been brought to an end. I had never spoken to Harold Wilson at length privately before, but this time we were alone except for Oliver Wright his private secretary, who did not speak, but took down notes of our discussion. I found the Prime Minister a good listener, quick-witted, polite, relaxed and extremely confident.

My second private meeting with the Prime Minister was on 8 December when I reported to him about discussions which I had had with President Nyerere. The following day I sent him a letter – which I quote in full – in which I set out at his request the matters which we had discussed.

9 December 1965

Dear Prime Minister,

It was very kind of you to find time to see me at such length yesterday afternoon, and I write to confirm the details of my conversation with President Nyerere, and my views on the Rhodesia situation.

1. The essence of the matter is to convince Nyerere that the British Government is determined to bring down the illegal Smith regime. Arthur Bottomley failed to do this, Malcolm MacDonald and I had some success, but Nyerere is still not wholly convinced. To persuade him of our firmness of purpose should be our top diplomatic priority.

2. Nyerere now recognizes that the time-table for toppling Smith by 15 December is ridiculous. He has shifted his ground by saying that he will require to be satisfied by 15 December that Britain means business.

3. He believes that British troops should be stationed in Zambia, both to protect Zambia and ultimately to enter Rhodesia. I sought to persuade him that no British Government could survive sending troops into Rhodesia until the Smith regime is crumbling, and there is a civil war mentality amongst the Europeans. When such a rift occurs, and assuming it percolates through the civil service, the police and the army, then the Governor would be justified in asking

British troops to enter Rhodesia to re-establish law and order. I told Nyerere that the timing for this state of affairs could not be accurately predicted, and this was why economic sanctions must first take their course.

4. Nyerere asked me what the British Government intended for Rhodesia when UDI was ended. I replied that I envisaged the establishing of colonial rule under the Governor working through a nominated executive council. For this to be achieved, it is my belief that the 1961 Constitution should be suspended. An attempt to revert to the 1961 Constitution raises the internal problem of how one would get a parliamentary majority through which the Government could function, and the external problem of giving Britain responsibility without power, which has been our prime weakness in all the negotiations with successive Rhodesian Governments, and has exposed us to great criticism at the United Nations and throughout the African continent. Nyerere, for his part, replied that he and other African leaders at least understood colonial rule, they had all been through it, and even though they had not liked it, they understood and even trusted the various processes which take place between Governor's rule and full independence.

5. It is important to distinguish between African short-term impatience to see Smith fall, and their long-term patience and understanding of Britain's role if exerted in bringing Rhodesia through the necessary stages to full independence based upon majority rule. I am convinced that Commonwealth African countries would, for the most part, give Britain between five and ten years to achieve this end. This is certainly what Nyerere said to me.

6. I had a talk with Colin Legum in Dar-es-Salaam, who had flown in that day from Salisbury. He said that the Governor, Beadle, Welensky and Evan Campbell, were all in favour of stronger sanctions and thought that we should invoke Chapter 7 of the United Nations Charter to make these mandatory. Welensky, in particular, had said that at an appropriate time we should make use of the threat of force. However, all those people apparently believe that after Smith has fallen we should revert to the 1961 Constitu-

tion. I believe this to be wrong for the reasons which I have already stated.

7. I believe Nyerere could be given a life-line which would dissuade him from breaking off diplomatic relations. It would not, in my view, be necessary to give a secret commitment to the use of force based on a time-table. I think it would suffice to spell out in greater detail the circumstances in which the British troops might enter Rhodesia, as described in number 3 of this letter. If Nyerere or any other Commonwealth government were nevertheless to break off diplomatic relations with this country, I am strongly of the view that we should take this calmly. We should say that we see no reason why they should remove their High Commissioner from London, and we should certainly not interrupt our programme of aid. If we are convinced that Smith can be brought down, those countries which have broken with us will wish to restore diplomatic relations rapidly and they should be allowed to do so. It would be immensely damaging for the Western position in Africa if in the meantime they were to start shopping around for aid with the Eastern bloc, in an endeavour to make up for what they have lost from us. This is the key to what occurred in Zanzibar immediately after the revolution. We shall in any event require the goodwill of all Commonwealth African countries in the immediate post-UDI period, and this could be jeopardized by unnecessary and precipitous action following upon their own childish decision to break with this country.

8. I cannot emphasize too strongly the need for discussions with African leaders on this issue, to be conducted by people who have known them well over the years. In this respect Maurice Foley is in a unique position and his personal contribution could be decisive in establishing a belief in Britain's sincerity.

I hope you will forgive this very lengthy letter, and the fact that I have now taken up so much of your time on two separate occasions. I have spent the greater part of the last six years in trying to establish understanding and friendship between Britain and African leaders during the stages of colonialism. I am sure that when the Rhodesian problem is settled, Britain and the new countries in Africa can have a most fruitful relationship. It is because I care most deeply about this matter that I venture to give you my views.

Yours sincerely,

HUMPHRY BERKELEY

I noted that shortly afterwards he followed my advice and sent Maurice Foley out to Zambia with Cledwyn Hughes to see Kenneth Kaunda. One of the weaknesses of the Labour Government at that time was that Arthur Bottomley knew the African scene but seemed neither convincing nor coherent in his public utterances, while Cledwyn Hughes, the Minister of State at the Commonwealth Office, was a complete newcomer to Africa.

I had a further encounter with William Whitelaw our Chief Whip on the evening of my second meeting with the Prime Minister. I told him I had seen Harold Wilson earlier that day. He immediately accused me of disloyalty. I flared up 'How dare you speak to me like that. I do not permit an accusation of disloyalty from a party functionary when I speak to the Prime Minister about a colony in rebellion.' His jaw dropped. I demanded an instant apology which he gabbled out. Sir John Vaughan Morgan who was sitting with us said to me, as Whitelaw retreated visibly shaken at the violence of my reaction, 'You have killed any chance you had of promotion'. As it happens I had only three more months of my parliamentary career ahead of me, but I did not care. Looking back on this incident I think I over-reacted to Whitelaw. But I was sick of the prevarication of the Conservative leadership on Rhodesia, and I resented the accusation of disloyalty from the Chief Whip of a Party, many of whose leaders were themselves conniving at an actual rebellion. When I saw Heath he was perfunctory and monosyllabic, and clearly thought my views on Africa were valueless.

I visited Rhodesia in January 1966 and saw for myself the nature of the Police State which by then existed. The newspapers were censored, my telephone was tapped. I delivered a note to Sir Humphrey Gibbs at Government House since his telephone had been disconnected. The following morning when

I was in my bath the telephone rang in my bedroom. It was the Governor's son speaking from downstairs. He had a letter for me from his father. I asked him to leave it with the porter. He firmly insisted upon bringing it up to my room. I draped a towel round me and let him in. He apologized for calling at such an obviously inconvenient moment, but said that if he had left the letter with the porter I would have not have received it since the Special Branch had taken over the porter's desk at Meikles Hotel.

The Governor asked me round for a drink. When I arrived I was received by his loyal ADC; and when the Governor entered the room the ADC shouted out 'Mr Humphry Berkeley—His Excellency the Governor'. It sounded slightly incongruous in the large, almost servantless, Government House. The Governor was accompanied by Sir Hugh Beadle who did most of the talking. Sir Humphrey seemed a simple, honourable man stunned and saddened by what had happened. Sir Hugh was a tubby little man with a bristling moustache, mobile eyes and an excessively ugly Rhodesian accent. He would hardly let Sir Humphrey open his mouth, and when the Governor did speak Beadle would interrupt to explain what his Excellency really meant. Sir Hugh told me that Smith had ordered the police to arrest the Governor and himself but that the Chief of Police had refused. I revealed this piece of information at a press conference which I gave in Salisbury, without giving away my source. Smith issued an indignant but lengthy denial, and I was subsequently declared a prohibited person by the Smith regime. When Beadle defected nearly three years later I reflected that the Governor cannot have been entirely unrelieved to have Government House to himself again even though he was to leave it before long.

Shortly after I returned to England Harold Wilson decided to hold a General Election and I lost my seat. I did not however lose my interest in Africa. At about this time stories were circulating about the possibility of my being appointed British High Commissioner to Zambia. This rumour appeared in several diary paragraphs and some time later it was suggested in some newspapers that I had been offered the post by Harold Wilson and turned it down.

The facts are as follows. I saw Anthony Greenwood – who was in the Cabinet as Minister of Overseas Development – shortly after the election, and he mentioned the possibility, asking if I would be interested in the post. I said that I would in principle, and he told me some years later that he had immediately written to the Prime Minister suggesting this appointment and had also spoken to some of his Cabinet colleagues—who had been enthusiastic. While I know that the appointment was suggested to the Prime Minister in this way, the Prime Minister never discussed the matter with me or even hinted that he had considered making it. I visited Zambia in July 1966 and had lunch with Kenneth Kaunda who greeted me with the words 'Well, Humphry, is the good news true, that you are coming to us as High Commissioner?' I said that I had heard the rumour too, but that as far as I knew there was nothing in it.

Although immediately after my election defeat I had shown interest in the post, long before the appointment of a new High Commissioner was made I realized that I would not be suitable and I took steps to see that the Prime Minister got to hear this. I would have undertaken the task of rebuilding the relationship between this country and Zambia with zest if I could have been assured that there would be no settlement of the Rhodesia problem except on the basis of majority rule. However, I was deeply opposed to a settlement on the basis of the *Tiger* or *Fearless* proposals which I regarded as being a complete sell-out to Smith. I would have felt bound to resign when negotiations were started on this basis, let alone if they were concluded. Harold Wilson quite legitimately tried on two occasions to achieve a settlement with Smith on a basis which most people in Britain would have supported, but which I could not. It would have made relations between him and Kenneth Kaunda even more delicate if his own High Commissioner had resigned within a few weeks of being appointed. I felt that I could play a useful unofficial role by carrying messages from one to the other from time to time, and explaining as best I could to each the problems and worries which the other had to face. When Kenneth Kaunda paid a visit to London in July 1968, Harold Wilson invited me to

10 Downing Street
Whitehall

July 12, 1968

PRIVATE AND
CONFIDENTIAL

Dear Humphry,

I was interested to receive your letter of July 8 about your talk with President Nyerere and have noted what you say in it.

George Thomson has told me of his own correspondence with you on the same subject. This is just to say that I fully share the view he has expressed in his letter to you of July 10.

I was indeed glad that Julius told you he would come to the next Commonwealth Prime Ministers' Conference, which, as you will have seen, is now to take place here in London during January. I shall much look forward to seeing him then.

Meanwhile, I also look forward to seeing you next week when we entertain Kenneth Kaunda.

Yours,
Harold Wilson

Humphry Berkeley, Esq.

the dinner party which he gave for the President at 10 Downing Street, and in his speech of welcome to Kenneth Kaunda he paid a very generous and undeserved tribute to the part which I had played in bringing them together. While there are obvious advantages in political appointments for top diplomatic posts in certain cases, I believe that the Prime Minister was correct in appointing to Zambia a highly-disciplined career civil servant.

When I became Chairman of the United Nations Association in November 1966 my first letter was addressed to Harold Wilson asking him to be the principal speaker at our Annual Conference. He accepted my invitation and he was my guest at a small dinner party in Manchester before the meeting. He also came to a drinks party which I gave for the members of UNA's Executive Committee afterwards. During dinner we had a long talk, mainly about Rhodesia. The Prime Minister told me that he had finally become convinced that Smith was a pathological liar during the *Tiger* talks. He told me then of the two incidents which he described in his recent memoirs: how Smith pretended that he had not received the Queen's invitation to lunch; and how Smith told Menzies that the Prime Minister would not see Smith, when in fact they had met the previous day. Harold Wilson also said that his own doctor, whom he had taken on board the *Tiger*, had come to a similar conclusion having observed Smith for several days. At the party after his speech I noticed for the first time the gregarious nature of Harold Wilson—he had something to say to every single person in the room. He was catching the night sleeper back to London but his staff had booked a room at the Midland Hotel so that he could work before returning to London. They kept on trying to get him away, but he refused to go. He said that he was enjoying himself, and it was only some minutes before his train was due to leave that he was finally dragged away.

A police officer said that his car would leave through the back entrance of the university because there were some anti-Vietnam students in the front. 'Nonsense', he replied. 'Come along Humphry, let us go and meet them.' He ran to the front of the building followed by his secretaries, myself, detectives and the police. He plunged straight into the gathering, answering their questions; asking his secretary to take down names and addresses so that further answers could be sent; and finally left in a burst of cheers.

Some months later I asked Harold Wilson if he would agree to hold a dinner at 10 Downing Street for me to launch an appeal for funds for the work of UNA. He agreed, and in April 1968 the Prime Minister presided over a dinner attended by Edward Heath and Jeremy Thorpe. There were forty-seven guests and on this one evening we raised £252,000, including a £10,000 cheque which the Prime Minister presented to me, the first instalment of a Government Grant which I had negotiated on behalf of UNA from George Brown. Again, since we sat next to each other during dinner, we had a lengthy talk. He recounted to me the dramas of George Brown's nine resignations which he has now made public. He was finally determined not to be rushed into a Cabinet reshuffle. 'Why do you suppose that I kept Michael Stewart on as First Secretary of State with no departmental duties? So that he was a Foreign Secretary in reserve, of course.' At one point he looked down the table and pointed at George Thomas, Minister of State at the Commonwealth Office. 'He's a good man', he said. I was not surprised when the following week George Thomas entered the Cabinet as Secretary of State for Wales. Again I was astonished at his resilience. For about two hours after dinner he moved from group to group sparkling like a diamond. It was shortly after some quite spectacularly bad by-election results but he did not appear to have a care in the world. By contrast Heath stood in a corner alone. I asked two members of UNA's staff to take people up to him, but whenever I turned round he seemed to be alone again. One would have supposed that these captains of industry would have wished to talk to the next Conservative Prime Minister, and he to them—but apparently not.

Harold Wilson has a spontaneous wit. On that evening Joe Hyman was the last to go. On the way out Hyman accused me of attacking Wilson in my book *The Power of the Prime Minister*. 'Humphry did not attack me', said the Prime Minister rather sharply. 'You are the greatest Prime Minister since

Walpole and you have no rivals', said Hyman ingratiatingly. 'You've forgotten the War of Jenkins's Ear' flashed back the Prime Minister with a gesture in the direction of his neighbour in No. 11. Another time before the fall of George Brown when Harold and Mary Wilson and I were receiving the guests at a UN Ball, it was clear that we were in for a rowdy evening. Large numbers of inebriated young men queued up to be received by us. It got noisier and noisier and suddenly we heard the sound of bagpipes. 'It sounds as though the Foreign Secretary has arrived' the Prime Minister whispered in my ear.

I will not disguise that I like Harold Wilson very much. As Prime Minister he had many faults; they were faults in a Prime Minister but not necessarily in a man. He is personally exceptionally kind. He hates sacking people, particularly loyal friends—he kept Arthur Bottomley and Fred Lee in the Government for far too long. He is exceptionally optimistic, always expecting the Smith regime to fall, or an economic miracle. He can be cocky but never arrogant, over-confident but never pompous. He likes power and believes that the Labour Party ought to be a party of power. He often underrates his opponents. He always underrated Edward Heath. Like R. A. Butler he believes that politics is the art of the possible, and he would never have taken on half the Labour Party to have clause 4 expunged as Gaitskell did. This may be politically less admirable, but it is also less damaging to yourself and your party.

Charges of dishonesty, deviousness, lack of principle and political opportunism have been levelled at Harold Wilson both during and since his period as Prime Minister. I would acquit him of dishonesty. What appears to be deviousness derives, I believe, from two of his shortcomings. He finds it difficult to take decisions and until 18 June 1970 was always bouncily and unreasoningly optimistic. Harold Wilson's approach to politics has always been pragmatic and unkindly critics can always equate this with lack of principle. He is certainly a political pragmatist. This is not necessarily a bad quality. It is part of the equipment of every politician. In Wilson's case his opportunism leads him to think of tomorrow's newspaper headlines rather than how his action may be judged in two or three years' time. It is his playing for the short-term advantage which has led many people to say that Wilson lacks credibility.

Harold Wilson has received condemnation and abuse for his attitude towards the Common Market. Many people have accused him of a political somersault. I do not believe that this charge can be sustained. A careful examination of the small print of what he said when he was Prime Minister makes it clear that his subsequent line as Opposition Leader is not inconsistent with his earlier speeches. It may be that he should have made his position even more clear when he was Prime Minister. I had hoped that Harold Wilson would in 1971 have come out in favour of Common Market entry. It must however be remembered that the Labour Party in Opposition is much more difficult to lead than the Conservative Party. It is much less disciplined, just as it is more easily torn apart. Its Party Conference and National Executive have far more authority. It is clear that both bodies are opposed to Britain's entry on the present terms. This cannot be ignored by a leader who faces re-election every year. The Conservative Party Conference is merely advisory. The Executive Committee of the National Union is a large cumbersome body which rarely discusses policy. Traditionally policy is laid down by the Leader and while dissenting grumbles are not unknown his decision is final.

I believe that Harold Wilson is trying to ensure that neither the National Executive nor the Party Conference will demand that the next Labour Government will withdraw from the Community. This is a thankless task and he will be much criticized, but I believe that he will succeed.

Harold Wilson has often been called a calculating man. Many people when accusing him of this mean that the public seldom see the real Harold Wilson and that he reacts to events in a particularly crafty and cunning way. This led to the feeling until June 1970 that he was politically invincible. I believe him to be much more straightforward than this. He shares with Quintin Hogg alone, among contemporary politicians, the instinct to capture the mood of the nation and rise to the occasion triumphantly. He also shares with Hogg the capacity to misjudge a situation disastrously. His dog licence speech was an example of such a misjudgment. He possesses to a high degree, as does Quintin Hogg, the qualities of courage and resilience which are essential for his temperament.

If Harold Wilson has learned the lesson of his defeat in 1970 when his weaknesses – over-confidence, optimism to the point of euphoria, and cockyness – were to the fore; and if he has learned that it is not necessary to score every tactical point however small in order to win a battle, he could become a great Prime Minister. After all, as he once said, a week in politics is a long time.

Chapter 12

Private Members Bills

There are, and I suppose there always will be, issues of social reform which cut across party barriers. Since these issues are traditionally described as matters of conscience they are not normally subject to a party whip. A government would not normally introduce a measure into the House of Commons unless it could be satisfied that it would be assured of a majority through all its stages. It is for this reason that private members bills are the normal parliamentary vehicle for this kind of reform. In recent years there have been four such measures: the abolition of hanging, homosexual law reform, abortion law reform, and divorce law reform. It is remarkable that all these measures should have passed through Parliament between 1964 and 1970 when a Labour Government was in power.

Although it is true that these issues do to some extent split the parties, it is nevertheless the case that the Labour Party is more solidly in favour of reform and the Conservative Party, on balance, is in favour of leaving the law as it is. This was particularly so in the case of the Abolition of the Death Penalty Bill of 1964 and the Bill to reform the laws relating to homosexuality of 1966. Perhaps this is inevitable since the Labour Party is traditionally in favour of reform.

After the Labour Party was returned to power in the General Election of October 1964 the new Government decided to give time to Mr Sidney Silverman's Bill to abolish capital punishment. This was an extremely important concession by the Government since many private members bills fail to become law through lack of time. By providing Government time for this Bill the Labour Government showed that it adopted an attitude of benevolent neutrality towards the measure.

Mr Sidney Silverman, then the Labour Member for Nelson and Colne, was anxious to obtain all-party sponsorship for his Bill, and he asked me to become a sponsor. I accepted his invitation, and my name appeared immediately after his as the second of twelve sponsors when the Bill was published. I had no hesitation in supporting the Bill—I had been opposed to hanging since my adolescence. I did not believe hanging to be a deterrent and this belief has been vindicated since the number of murders has not in fact varied appreciably since the death penalty was abolished in 1965.

The number of murders in this country has remained extraordinarily constant during the last forty years. Since 1930 there have never been less than 130 and never more than 200 murders in any single year. As a proportion of the population these figures are statistically insignificant. Roughly half the known muderers commit suicide subsequently and plainly are not, therefore, deterred at the thought of hanging. A high proportion of those apprehended are found unfit to plead. It happens that in 1964 the penalties relating to murder were in a thoroughly confused and unsatisfactory state. Owing to the compromise measure which Mr Heath forced through Parliament when he was Chief Government Whip (one of the rare occasions when a whip has been used for this kind of measure) the conclusions of a Royal Commission that there should not be two degrees of murder were ignored. Capital punishment was retained, for example, for murder by shooting, but not for murder by poisoning. The number of people hanged in the last three years before the death penalty was abolished was two a year.

For some reason the issue of hanging has always aroused strong emotions in the Conservative Party. Many members of the Lancaster Conservative Association were strongly critical of my decision to sponsor and vote for Sidney Silverman's Bill. I recall a public meeting when a Conservative member of the Lancaster City Council asked me what the state could do with all the murderers who would have been hanged and would now, under the proposed Bill, be reprieved. He seemed to think that the number involved ran into many thousands and that if the Bill were passed a major programme of prison construction would be necessary. He flatly refused to believe me when I told him that only six people had been hanged during the last three years. He sank back to his seat shouting, 'You can prove anything by statistics.'

I remember the hanging of Derek Bentley in 1953. Bentley and Craig were both charged with the crime of murder and were both found guilty. Craig was not hanged since he was under 16 years of age. Bentley, although only two years older, was hanged. He had not used a gun, and the only real evidence against him was that he shouted to Craig 'Let them have it, Chris'. Craig was armed and Bentley was not and it was at least arguable that what Bentley meant was that Craig should surrender his weapon. Bentley denied that he even said this.

I shall never forget the following day. I was in the Carlton Club shortly before lunch and was watching the news tape machine in the entrance. Shortly afterwards Sir David Maxwell-Fyfe, then the Home Secretary, entered the Club looking white and exhausted, as well he might since Bentley had been hanged that morning. Suddenly a group of Club members appeared carrying their whiskeys and dry martinis in their hands and clapped Sir David on the back with shouts of 'Well done, David'.

At that moment I hated the Conservative Party. They treated the hanging of a nineteen-year-old boy with the jubilation which would normally attend a bump supper at Oxford or Cambridge. Sir David, who was one of the kindest men whom I have ever met, obviously was repelled by the demonstration too.

It was with this incident in mind that I posed in 1969 my much quoted question 'Do you teach the Labour Party economics, or the Tory Party to be humane?'

In fact Silverman's Bill was passed with a comfortable majority. Only one Labour MP voted against it, Mr Frank Tomney. Ninety or so Conservatives voted in favour of the reform; some of them wobbled after pressure from their constituents but the number was few.

I had a more difficult decision to take on 26 May 1965. This arose on the Committee Stage of the Bill. A clause had been moved by Mr Henry Brooke which had the effect of abolishing the death penalty, but only for a five-year experimental period. As I said in the debate:

> Having heard speeches from both sides of the Committee, I recognize that I am pulled in both directions. I have decided to support the clause, because although I believe that the case for abolition is an overwhelming one and that the next five years will show that there has been no perceptible increase in the murder rate, I also believe that Parliament should have an opportunity of considering in five years' time what has been the effect of this measure.

I felt that those of us who had rested our case upon our belief that the murder rate would not increase as the result of abolition should have our beliefs put to the test. Despite a strong campaign by Mr Duncan Sandys abolition became permanent four years later, a year earlier than had been intended, and it was conclusively shown that the murder rate had not increased as a result of the abolition of the death penalty.

In November 1965 I drew second place in the ballot for private members bills, having balloted in the previous six years without success. Pressure is put upon back-bench MPs to take part in the ballot by the Whips on both sides in the hope that at least some of the successful members will belong to their own party.

I was informed that I had drawn the second place by the Deputy Speaker, Sir Samuel Storey, with whom I shared a taxi from the House of Commons to the Carlton Club on 18 November 1965. I was determined to use the occasion, which guaranteed a certain and early debate, for an important social measure. By the end of lunch I had decided to use the opportunity to introduce into the House of Commons a measure which had already been introduced into the House of Lords by Lord Arran which, in effect, implemented the recommendations of the Wolfenden Committee on homosexual law reform.

I knew this would be controversial. I was prepared for the barrage of abusive and anonymous letters which I received, although they were outnumbered by ten to one by letters of support, including one from the Archbishop of Canterbury. I could not have foreseen that my Bill would be read for a second time on 11 February 1966—only six weeks before polling day in the 1966 General Election. I had sponsors from all parties, and my close friend Christopher Chataway agreed to wind up the debate from our side. For the first time ever the House of Commons voted in favour of homosexual law reform. 164 voted in favour of the Bill and 107 voted against. Only a year previously the House of Commons had voted against the same issue. My Bill would undoubtedly have become law had a General Election not taken place. As it was, Leo Abse added it to his already lengthy list of unpopular causes, and it became law in the next Parliament.

I have no doubt that my promotion of this Bill cost me my seat. Lancaster went Labour by a swing of 6 per cent, twice the national average.

Shortly after the election I met one of my former Conservative parliamentary colleagues, a personal friend, in Kuwait. 'Never mind', he said comfortingly though a trifle insensitively, 'in ten years' time everybody will have forgotten about that wretched Bill.'

I do not want anybody to forget about it. I am more proud of introducing the Sexual Offences Bill than of anything else that I did or said in six and a half years as a Member of the House of Commons. Here was one sphere where a back-bench MP could do what no Government would have the courage to do. Since the arguments have not changed, I make no apology for reproducing the main body of my speech. I could not state the case more clearly today.

'As the principal sponsor of the Bill, I recognize that it is a controversial Measure and that it arouses strong feelings, either in support or against, on both sides of the House. There are hon. Members, as there are members of the public, who would prefer that we did not consider legislation on this subject at the present time. There are even some who regret the fact that we are inquiring into what many people believe to be one of the pressing social issues of our time.

'To people who feel like this, I would say only that it was recognized by a Conservative Home Secretary in 1954 that the subject of homosexuality was something about which far too little was known. It was recognized that it represented a major problem for society, and after the Wolfenden Committee was appointed it took about three years to hear and sift the evidence and ultimately to produce a report. This in itself, and the fact that the report was produced with only one dissentient, justifies our belief that after a lapse of eight years since the Committee reported the time is now ripe for legislation. . . .

'When we in this House have previously discussed or recommended legislation, it has frequently been the posture of those who resisted that the time was not yet right. Two successive Secretaries of State for the Home Department said as much as this—the present Lord Butler of Saffron Walden, when he was Secretary of State during 1958, and my right hon. Friend the Member for Hampstead (Mr Henry Brooke). It is interesting to note that neither suggested that the recommendations of the Wolfenden Committee were undesirable in themselves nor that they were contrary to public opinion. It was suggested instead that they were ahead of public opinion.

'In previous debates we have had on this subject, certain hon. Members have been inclined to resist the idea of a change in the law but have accepted the inevitability of a change at some time or another. The most notable case is my right hon. Friend the Member for Ashford (Mr W. F. Deedes), who last took part in a discussion on the Wolfenden recommendations in a debate initiated by the present Minister of Health in 1960.

'I recognize that, in addition to many Members of this House who have hitherto felt that the time for a change in the law was inopportune, there may be others who feel most strongly and sincerely that the changes outlined in this Bill are undesirable. I recognize that, and I recognize the sincerity with which they feel this. In turn, I hope they will recognize the sincerity of the motives of the sponsors of this Bill for believing that the changes in the law which we are proposing are desirable.

'I said "the motives of the sponsors of this Bill" because it will not surprise hon. Members to know that those who are sponsoring this Bill and myself as the principal sponsor, have had a very large correspondence on this subject. As one would expect, the vast bulk of the letters to me, and I think to other sponsors, from people opposed to this Bill, are abusive, anonymous and attack our integrity and our motives. I am glad that no one in this House would wish to do that. . . .

'Public opinion is not unimportant in these matters, because successive Secretaries of State have stressed the need to carry the public with the Government before any change in the law can be brought about. Although I am not greatly enamoured of public opinion polls, and I think that Members of Parliament of all people should not be mesmerized by them, it is worth noting that in recent months a Gallup poll and National Opinion poll have been taken on whether the public believe that a change in the law on the lines of the Wolfenden proposals is desirable.

'Curiously enough, in both cases, 63 per cent. of those who were polled supported a change in the law along the lines of the Wolfenden proposals, which are the lines upon which this Bill has been based. Those who object to this Bill merely on the grounds that public opinion is not yet ready for a change in the law may wish to reconsider their attitude in the light of these polls which have recently been published. I would like to give certain reasons why the sponsors of the Bill believe that not only is it timely for the law to be changed, in terms of public opinion, but also why we believe fundamentally that a change in the law is necessary.

'Before the Wolfenden Committee produced its Report in 1957, there was a great deal of ignorance in this country about homosexuality, both about its causes and its prevalence and nature. Since then the question has been widely discussed, and other publications have also appeared, notably a publication by Mr Michael Schofield, which was sponsored to some extent by the Home Office and was part of the research promised by Lord Butler in 1960 when he resisted the idea of changing the law. A great deal more knowledge has become available to the public and hon. Members about this subject. Whereas ten or fifteen years ago most of us could have been properly excused for thinking that homosexuality was a practice carried on by people of unusually perverted morals who had the alternative of leading perfectly normal heterosexual lives but who deliberately chose a more vicious way of life as a matter of preference, this is now something in which it is no longer possible for us to believe in the light of the immense amount of evidence that has become available.

'One of the facts which all of us should bear in mind is that, although estimates are difficult to make with precise accuracy, it is generally believed that there are something like 5 per cent of the male population who are exclusively homosexual in their desires. That is, there are approximately 5 per cent of the males of this country who have normal sexual urges who are attracted solely and exclusively towards members of their own sex.

'This provides us with evidence which many of us would have lacked ten or fifteen years ago. It makes it clear that homosexuals have a choice. Anybody who suggests that they do not have a choice is wrong; but their choice is a harsh one, sterner and more brutal than many people imagine. The basic choice which they have is whether to be chaste or to commit homosexual acts. They do not have the choice, for the most part, of whether they should commit homosexual or heterosexual acts. This I believe to be absolutely fundamental in our thinking about the law on this subject.

'The second point which we should consider is this. On the evidence available – this is brought out particularly in Michael Schofield's book – the vast number of homosexuals who were subjected to interviews to prepare the material for this book passionately wanted to be heterosexual and disliked intensely their own physical condition. As far as one can see from the evidence, it seems likely that their condition was in-born rather than the result of corruption, and the degree of proselytization about which we have heard so much appears to have been greatly over-estimated.

'Those of us in the House who are practising members of the Christian faith – and I regard myself as one – are faced with something of a problem. All of us who are Christians, and probably many who are not, regard homosexual acts as morally wrong. On the other hand, all of us who are Christians, and many others, equally must have a feeling of compassion and justice for a minority of the population who find themselves in a condition for which they have no responsibility. It is important for us to recognize that it is not a crime in this country to be a homosexual. It is a crime in this country to commit homosexual acts, and nobody has suggested – and, as far as I know, none of the opponents of the Bill has suggested – that homosexuals are responsible for their condition.

'Let us see what the law as it stands does. If it is accepted that, say, 5 per cent of the males in this country are in a homosexual condition for which they have no responsibility, if it is accepted that homosexuals are likely to be as highly sexed in terms of desire as heterosexuals, we are giving this 5 per cent, who, let us face it, amount to about 1 million people, a stark choice; either they are chaste for their entire adult life, or they commit a single indiscretion and become criminals and liable to prosecution. We should recognize that this is what the law does and says.

'One of the other interesting facets of the information now available to us as a result of the Wolfenden Report and other data, particularly Michael Schofield's book, is that it removes what must have been a very prevalent view among most people who were ignorant about homosexuality, namely, that the average homosexual has a preference for young boys. As far as I can judge on the evidence which I have looked at, there is absolutely no evidence to show that homosexuals are more likely to be attracted by or to assault juveniles than heterosexuals. It is extremely important for us to recognize this point. I will come to the question of penalties, particularly in relation to minors, later. I believe that out of justice and compassion to a sizeable element in our population a change in the law is desirable.

'There are at least two other reasons, which may have a more widespread appeal particularly among those who, for perfectly honourable and natural reasons, find this a subject which they can consider only with revulsion, why we should contemplate a change in the law. The first is that at present the law is totally and completely unenforceable. Nobody has ever attempted to enforce it except in a most arbitrary way. If we assume that there are 1 million homosexuals in this country, and if we assume, therefore, that millions of homosexual acts take place every year – 50 or 60 million is the estimated figure given by Michael Schofield – and if we recognize that only 1,300 prosecutions take place, this makes the unenforceability of the law absolutely plain to everybody. If a law is completely unenforceable, and if nobody attempts to enforce it, it must be a bad law and must bring the law clearly into contempt.

'I should like to say something about what I understand to be the enforcement of the law. The vast bulk of the 1,300 prosecutions are not against consenting adults in private. For the most part, they are in respect of offences committed in public. They may be offences against byelaws. They may be offences of assault. They may be offences against minors. I think that every hon. Member believes that all of these should remain part of the law.

'There are, however, I understand, approximately 100 offences a year which are now illegal and which fall into three categories. There is the offence which is called the stale offence—that is, it took place over 12 months previously. There is the offence which comes to the notice of the police as a result of blackmail threats. There is the offence which the Bill seeks to make no longer an offence—an act committed in private by two consenting adults. I am told that the offences in these three categories add up to approximately 100 a year. By far the greater number of the millions of homosexual acts which we understand take place occur in private and would no longer be a crime of the law were changed and which even now are hardly ever prosecuted except in the most arbitrary fashion.

'I understand that in the last year or so there has been a change in attitude on the part of the prosecuting authorities towards certain categories of homosexual offences and that the Director of Public Prosecutions has invited chief constables to consult him on any homosexual offences which fall within this category of the 100—that is to say, blackmail, stale offences or offences committed by adults in private.

'I have heard it said – and that is why I wish to make the point clear – that chief constables have to secure the approval of the Director of Public Prosecutions before a prosecution is made for offences that fall within these three categories. This

I believe to be completely untrue. A chief constable has complete discretion as to whether to prosecute. In the case of offences concerning adults in private, the object of the Director of Public Prosecutions in making that request to chief constables was not, as many people think, to stop prosecutions altogether. It was merely to secure some sort of uniformity in prosecutions as between one police authority and another, and that is plainly desirable. In no case, however, can the Director of Public Prosecutions instruct a police officer not to prefer a charge.

'Those who say that there is not much need to change the law because prosecutions are very few and may well become fewer ignore two undesirable possibilities. The first is that the law is ignored, and that is always bad. The second, however, is that a category of people, namely, chief constables, are being given a power to defy the law of the country, a power which no Minister would dream of exercising. In fact, Ministers may be even less qualified than chief constables to exercise this power. It is thoroughly undesirable for a chief constable to do so either.

'It seems to me, therefore, that we have to make up our minds whether we believe it to be right and just that people should be prosecuted in private as consenting male adults. I do not believe that we can shirk this issue by simply saying that there is not much point in changing the law because very few of them are prosecuted. If that is the case, the law is bad; and if the law is bad, it must be changed. In terms of the public good, enforceability is an essential.

'The second point, which is far more horrifying, is the question of blackmail. It is easy to exaggerate both the amount of blackmail that homosexual offences arouse and, secondly, the amount of mitigation in terms of blackmail that a reform in the law would bring about. I have been interested to note, in my very large correspondence since my intention to publish the Bill became known, that a sizeable number of people who have written to me, most of whom, for obvious reasons, have been anonymous, have told me that they are victims of blackmail and that they are frightened to go to the police because they are not sure, if they go to the police, whether they will be able to prefer a charge against a blackmailer or whether the police will turn upon them and prosecute them for their offence.

'Again, I know that the object of the Director of Public Prosecutions in asking the police to consult him in blackmail cases was to give some sort of, if not undertaking, at least reassurance, to people that the State regarded blackmail as being a filthier crime than homosexual acts. Nevertheless, I believe that until that law is changed there will always be people who fear that they will be prosecuted as a result of a blackmail complaint.

'The interesting fact about the 100 people a year in the three categories which I have mentioned – stale offences, blackmail and consenting adults in private – is that there were 45 prosecutions, and those prosecutions, I am informed, included people who went to the police on a blackmail complaint. This may happen rarely, but it happens.

'It can be argued – and it was argued in another place – that the great fear of somebody who is being blackmailed is social disgrace, and that homosexual acts, even though they may cease to be a crime, will still be regarded by most people as being morally reprehensible. This I accept. It is true.

'What a change in the law would do, however, is this. If in future after the law has been changed a man is blackmailed, he will not hesitate to go to the police and the blackmailer will immediately be apprehended. If a prosecution takes place, the man who is being blackmailed, as is always the case in blackmail charges, will appear in court as Mr X. His identity will not become known and he will not be subject to prosecution by the police because he has not committed a criminal act. Therefore, although, obviously, one cannot eliminate blackmail or even, perhaps, reduce it as substantially as we would all like to see it reduced, this is bound to have an effect in reducing the element of blackmail in homosexual cases, which I believe to be one of the most unpleasant features of the state of law in relation to homosexuality. Those, it seems to me, are the basic arguments in favour of a reform in the law. . . .

'Basically, there are two principles behind the Bill. The first is that homosexual acts between consenting adults in private should no longer be subject to criminal penalties. The second, which is, perhaps, an amplification of the first, is that the age of consent should, we believe, be fixed at the age of 21.

'I should like to deal with both those objects briefly. In the first case, I was at one point under some temptation from certain hon. Members who have been extremely helpful concerning my Bill to restrict its scope to a straight abolition of the Labouchere Amendment. In the end, together with my co-sponsors, I decided that this would not be a satisfactory measure, for a variety of reasons.

'First, we came to the same conclusion as the Wolfenden Committee that there is no valid and overwhelming distinction between the act of buggery and other homosexual acts. I was reinforced in this view by the speeches made in another place by the Archbishop of Canterbury and the Archbishop of York. It seems to me that, if one were to keep the maximum sentence for buggery as life imprisonment and abolish all penalties for other homosexual acts, one would produce a conclusion which would hardly be justifiable on the grounds of either morality or common sense.

'We also decided that if buggery remained a criminal offence when committed between consenting adults in private, the unenforceability of the law would remain and the invasion of privacy, which is basically one's objection to the Labouchere Amendment, would not in any way be diminished. For these two reasons we decided to follow precisely the Wolfenden Recommendations on this point.

'This matter was discussed at great length in another place. It was pointed out by both Lord Dilhorne and Lord Kilmuir that, unlike other homosexual practices which have been criminal for only a short period of time – within the lifetime of many people alive today – that of buggery had been a crime for hundreds of years, dating from the Middle Ages and perhaps earlier. Until Tudor times at least it was an ecclesiastical crime, and came before the ecclesiastical courts. Were we to have ecclesiastical courts in 1966 buggery would not be a crime because the Churches, every one of them, in Britain are overwhelmingly in favour of amending the law on the lines of the Wolfenden proposals. . . .

'One should ponder on a state of affairs when a secular society, which is what we are, takes a harsher view in terms of morality than the Church itself. In medieval times the Church took a harsher view, and that is why buggery became an ecclesiastical crime.

'One of the objects of the Bill is to cease to make these offences a crime, while recognizing, as all Christians must, that they are grave sins. I hope that the House will now understand why the sponsors of the Measure have decided to follow the Wolfenden recommendations in relation to buggery.

'The age of 21 as the age of consent is something to which we attach a great deal of importance. If, as would appear to be the case, the homosexual condition is a form of emotional retardedness – and this is the most accurate description one can put on it – people who are vulnerable to pressures during adolescence must be protected. It is in some ways illogical that the age of consent for girls should be 16 and that it is perfectly legal to corrupt a young girl into female homosexual practices at the age of 16 while for men the age of consent should be 21.

'However, we feel that the age of consent for men should remain at 21, for two reasons. The first is because adolescence is a period of emotional instability and, therefore, protection should be given. The second is that whatever one may feel about the unpleasant nature of the physical acts involved, looking at the problem of homosexuality as a whole we see that it is the appalling emotional loneliness and frustration which leads to so many mental breakdowns. That is something for which we should offer all the protection society can to adolescents.

'It has been argued that we should raise the age of consent to 25, but we believe that 21 should remain the age. It is the age at which people achieve full responsibility and if we were to raise it further – to, say, 25 – it would not be satisfactory for a variety of reasons. . . . I have attempted to outline what I believe to be the motives of those of us who promote the Bill, and the reasons why it is socially desirable. I recognize, of course, that there are many people who are sincerely and honestly opposed to this Bill, and who believe that it would have disastrous consequences. To those people who are, as it were, irreconcilable in their opposition to this Measure, I would say that I hope that they will thank God each day of their lives that they do not belong to this 5 per cent of people who are exclusively attracted to their own sex, and who have, as far as we know, a normal sex urge.

'I hope that opponents of the Bill will reflect on the fact that those who have voluntarily undertaken to lead lives of chastity – namely, ordained priests and monks – as opposed to being compelled to do so by the present law – and I talk about celibates who may have heterosexual or homosexual inclinations; those who have taken this vow – are strongly in favour of a reform in the law. The reason why they are, perhaps, in favour of a reform in the law is that they know from their own experience as men of God that prayer, meditation, and the aid of the Sacraments to resist strong temptation are required in order to lead a life of absolute chastity from the start of the adult state until the grave. We should remember that this Measure is supported by people like that.

'I should also like to say to those people who are hoping that this Measure will go through that I can well recognize that there may be people who are far more suitable than myself to promote the Bill – I wish we could have found as promoter a father of 19 children – but I can say that I believe that the time for a change in the law is ripe, and that, having secured so favourable a position in the Ballot, it was my duty to introduce the Bill.'

I ended by saying: 'I was brought up by my father, who was himself a Member of this House, which he loved, to believe that being a Member of Parliament was one of the greatest honours one could have bestowed on one. But he also taught me that it was the duty of an MP to do what he thought was right regardless of the consequences to himself. In that mood, I commend this Bill to the House.'

These were the last words which I uttered as a Conservative Member of Parliament.

After the debate was over and the second reading of the Bill had been obtained, I received many letters from my colleagues, of which those from the Rt. Hon. Richard Wood, the present Minister of Overseas Development, and Tam

Dalyell, a Labour MP, were not untypical. They read as follows:

14 February 1966

My dear Humphry,

Thank you very much for your letter which it was a delight to get. You will probably agree that all politicians long for encouragement and very seldom get it, so your letter was a great joy.

You were kind to say that my speech had had an influence on the size of the victory. I think it would be much truer for me to say what a great many people recognize, that your own speech at the beginning not only set the whole tone of what I thought was a good debate, but also had the effect of persuading even your critics that this was an eminently reasonable case. It really was a splendid beginning and, when you sat down, I felt that victory was already assured!

Yours ever,

RICHARD

11 February 1966

Dear Humphry,

In charity and humanity, that was one of the remarkable speeches of my $3\frac{1}{2}$ years in the House of Commons. Though I am not one of the 5% and am happily married, I am deeply grateful for your brave stand.

You may recollect that I pleaded a prior engagement when you first approached me to be present. To their immense credit, the Reading Training College phoned me on Wednesday, 'We have gone to some trouble to arrange your meeting – Sir Edward Boyle has spoken already at the second meeting in our series for the Conservatives – but since we read that Humphry Berkeley is short of supporters on Friday, and since we believe that his proposals constitute vital social legislation, we would ask you to give us another date.'

I told them that I thought this reflected the maximum credit on them.

Good luck,

Yours sincerely,

TAM DALYELL

Chapter 13

Ambition and Office

The majority of Members of Parliament do not wish to sit on a back bench throughout their political lives. I was no exception. While the life of a back-bencher is useful and sometimes even exciting, it lacks the enthralling interest of administering a great department of state. Some of my Conservative colleagues were content to sit in the House for the almost statutory fifteen years which, in my time, preceded the granting of a knighthood. I had no such ambition; indeed had I been a Member of Parliament for fifteen years and been offered a knighthood, I would have regarded my political career as one of dismal failure.

Although I was unsympathetic to the career and personality of Sir Samuel Hoare, I echo his sentiments about political office as expressed in his book *Nine Troubled Years*. He wrote, 'The life of a private member had no attraction for me, except as a step on the stairway to the front bench'. It is, of course, much easier to want office than to get it. I have little doubt that I could have obtained junior office in the Conservative Party during my first Parliament had I behaved in the right way. I recall dining with the Government Chief Whip, then Mr Martin Redmayne, within a few weeks of my entry into Parliament. I remember him saying with some complacency, 'I am not called the Patronage Secretary for nothing', and feeling slightly sick.

In order to achieve office it is helpful to have a patron. It is wise to be serviceable to the Whips, to agree to speak in a certain way in a debate, or more frequently to agree not to speak in a debate in order to get through the business of the Government speedily. A little gentle sycophancy seldom comes amiss, particularly if this involves writing to a minister to congratulate him on a parliamentary performance in terms which are both extravagant and slightly breathless.

My trouble was that I was physically incapable of flattery or fawning. I could never join a group round Harold Macmillan or some other senior figure in the Party and laugh without restraint at their inferior jokes. Nor did I ever have much truck with the Whips. I recognize that political parties have to have Whips, but under Martin Redmayne with one or two exceptions, they were people of military bearing and limited intelligence. On one occasion I had to inform the Chief Whip that I was not prepared to have any further dealings with my own particular area Whip. I was sick of being spoken to in bullying blackmailing terms.

Needless to say, I was never offered a place in the Whips Office. I would not have accepted such an offer had it, improbably, been made. I believe that a prolonged spell in the Whips Office leads to a serious erosion of character. The constant need is to get Government business through as quickly as possible. Hence the greater part of a Whip's duties is to persuade his members to vote, often against their convictions. Whips employ a combination of bullying, blackmail and charm for this purpose. In their preoccupation of getting legislation through they frequently give too little thought to the nature of the measure itself. Not infrequently they use the wrong methods in dealing with individual members. I would, for example, react somewhat explosively towards bullying and blackmail. Yet these were the weapons most frequently employed in an attempt to keep me docile. Despite my distaste for Whips as a whole, I must make exceptions in the case of two of my own area Whips, Brian Batsford and Martin McLaren. Both of these were invariably courteous, considerate and civilized. Their behaviour was in marked contrast to the majority of their colleagues. I regard Mr Heath's eight years in the Whips Office and his four-year spell as Chief Whip as the worst possible qualification for a future Prime Minister.

I am not of course arguing that slobbering loyalty to the Party and its leaders is the only way to achieve office. Many members of the present Government, including Christopher Chataway, Lord Balniel, Ian Gilmour, Peter Kirk and Anthony

Lambton were strikingly independent when they were back-benchers. It is, however, the case that rebellion frequently does not pay off. I was never rebellious for the sake of being rebellious, let alone because I thought that this might prove to be my road to office. I like to think that there has been a consistency about my disagreements with the Conservative leadership which culminated in my leaving the Conservative Party. I was told by a member of the then Shadow Cabinet that I would have been offered junior office if Sir Alec Douglas-Home had won the election of 1964. I do not know whether this is true or not.

I have always wanted office because I feel that my talents lie in the fields of administration and decision-making. I should particularly like to have been a Minister in the Foreign and Commonwealth Office. It could be argued, and no doubt has been, that my maverick quality, or as I prefer to term it, my robust independence makes me unsuitable for ministerial office because I would always be wanting to resign. I am not a resigner by nature although I do not find it easy to be in a subordinate position. I have in fact a very clear idea about the sort of issue upon which a minister should resign.

Had I been a Home Office minister in the last Labour Government, I should have resigned over the East African Asian legislation. The position of Mr David Ennals was in my view quite indefensible. He was completely opposed to the measure. Yet as Under-Secretary at the Home Office, he was defending it day by day at the Dispatch Box. His explanation to me that he could exert more influence if he stayed in the Government was contemptible and I told him so at the time. Although I was equally opposed to the Bill, I would not have thought it necessary to resign if I had been a minister in another government department totally unconnected with the measure.

If Harold Wilson had reached an agreement with the rebel Smith regime on the basis of the *Tiger* or *Fearless* proposals, I should have resigned from the Government no matter what post I held. I should have done so because this would have been a complete betrayal of the five million Africans in Rhodesia and would set in train a sequence of events in Southern Africa of which I wholly disapproved. A minister must always be prepared to resign, and without any regard for his political future. There are many cases of a political comeback of which Harold Wilson and Anthony Eden are merely two examples. Others who include Duff Cooper and Sir Thomas Dugdale never regained their political base. It is sometimes a disadvantage never to have resigned. Perhaps if R. A. Butler had resigned at one point during his twenty-six years of office, he would have become Prime Minister. Perhaps the continual and inevitable compromises which anybody would be forced to accept in a ministerial career which lasted so long had made him soft.

There is no doubt that in the public mind at any rate the ethics of politicians appear to have degenerated during the last twenty or thirty years. When my father sat in Parliament fifty years ago, politics was thought to be an honourable profession. When I entered the House in 1959, MPs were not regarded as being beneath contempt. Today I sense that my non-political friends regard all save a few politicians as being venal, corrupt and time-serving. I have become a little weary of being introduced as one of the few politicians who has stuck to his principles. I do not believe the statement to be true. All that I have done is to speak my mind a trifle more stridently than some of my contemporaries, many of whom have principles and standards of behaviour which are higher than mine.

Nevertheless it would be foolish to ignore the fact that disillusionment with politicians and the established political parties in this country has reached such a pitch that our entire fabric of democratic government is at risk. Politicians are widely regarded as being dishonest and their promises are thought to be meaningless. I have outlined certain remedies which are designed to shift back some power from the Executive to the Legislature – that is to say from Whitehall to Westminister – in my previous book *The Power of the Prime Minister.* While I would alter some of the details of the ailment which I described in 1968 I would not alter the main diagnosis nor the cure which I prescribed.

If, like myself, you still seek a career in politics you must accept that you have an obligation to describe your motivation as truthfully as possible. Most politicians are rather odd people.

Those, like Stanley Baldwin, who appear to be the most normal are in fact the oddest. Most politicians are simultaneously cynical and idealistic, self-centred and disinterested, candid and cunning. They are susceptible to the grossest flattery; they rival actors in their sustained ability to talk about themselves and ruthlessly to wrench any discussion into an examination of their ego and its relationship to the matter being discussed. I recognize all these qualities in myself.

In many cases they are jealous of their contemporaries. This feeling I have fought and overcome. Jealously is poison. If you are embarked upon an enterprise where the stakes are as extreme as Downing Street or the gutter, you must rid your system of poison.

I do not in fact believe that politicians are any less honest or moral than they were fifty or a hundred years ago. Two happenings have occurred which have made their lives immeasurably more difficult. They are responsible to a mass electorate and Britain has undergone, in my lifetime, a reduction in her international power which is only comparable to the destruction of the Ottoman and Austro-Hungarian Empires earlier in the century.

The responsibility to a mass electorate has inevitably debased the coinage of political controversy if only because simplification often involves distortion. I doubt whether any politician could go through an election campaign without at some time making a political speech of which, were it not for the merciful shortness of memory, he would subsequently be ashamed. Some politicians are incapable of making any other sort of speech.

No other nation has gone from being top country in the world to a small to medium-size power within a generation and retained the democratic process. Since 1945 each Prime Minister on departure has left Britain a weaker country than when he came into office. In few cases has the Prime Minister been to blame although the shock to the nation administered by Sir Anthony Eden in 1956 started a national nervous breakdown from which we have not yet fully recovered.

I have already proclaimed my faith in Britain's active participation in the United Nations, Europe, and our multiracial Commonwealth. I regard Mr Heath's references to our return to greatness when Britain goes into Europe as meaningless jingoism. His statement that Britain will not be pushed around any more by her Commonwealth friends gives the the impression of an indignant housewife being jostled in a supermarket rather than a determined resolve to find our proper role which can and should be moral leadership rather than military strength or material well-being.

I voted Labour in June 1970. I took this decision because the Conservative leadership was committed to the sale of arms to South Africa. I knew that this would endanger the future of the Commonwealth. Mr Heath was also committed to a further series of talks with Mr Ian Smith. I knew that the prospects of an honourable settlement did not exist in any discussions with the Rhodesia Front. I was affronted when the Conservative Leaders, with the exception of Sir Edward Boyle, supported the South African cricket tour on the grounds that sporting contacts with South Africa might bring about a change of heart among its White ruling class. All the evidence pointed to the opposite conclusion.

I wrote an article in the *Guardian* in May 1970 – before it was known that an immediate General Election was likely – announcing that I had decided to vote Labour at the election whether it was to take place in the spring or the autumn. I wrote to Harold Wilson in July 1970 in the aftermath of Labour's defeat and asked to join the Party. I was admitted in October. I am glad that I should have joined Labour in defeat; I could have joined the Party when it was still the Government. At least nobody can justly accuse me of political opportunism.

My reasons for joining the Labour Party have not always been fully understood. I remember a conversation which I had in August 1970 with Miss Joan Wicken, the British Personal Assistant to President Nyerere of Tanzania and a life-long Socialist. I was rather startled at the vehemence of her reproach—'Why did you have to join the Labour Party, why couldn't you have joined the Liberals. Labour is too diluted already.' I had at least supposed that someone as closely aware of my views on Britain and Southern Africa and as involved herself in these matters might have comprehended. I was also vain enough to believe that the Labour Party might benefit from the kind of dilution that I could provide.

I knew of course that I would have been made welcome in the Liberal Party. Mr Jeremy Thorpe publicly stated this when I left the Consevative Party in 1968. I was less certain of my reception in the Labour Party. Yet I was never tempted to join the Liberals for reasons which I must explain.

It would be very venal to join a major party in the expectation that it would, at some time, be returned to power, rather than to join a more congenial small party doomed indefinitely to the frustrations of opposition. The Liberal Party, however, has never seemed to me to have a wholly credible or coherent policy. I pay tribute to its foresight in consistently pioneering the cause of European unity when the major parties were indifferent or blind to the part that Britain could play in this direction. I also revere the Liberal tradition in British politics to which my father made some contribution. Nevertheless, remoteness from power has made the Liberal vote one of constant protest and this in turn has given a certain raggedness to proclaimed Liberal policy. Not only has the Liberal Party no prospect of power, but I do not believe that it any longer has the power to influence, in the smallest degree, the course of events in this country. For this reason I believe that a radical, such as myself, is more likely to find a base for action within the Labour Party.

I am certainly not a Marxist but I believe that we should strive to achieve a greater measure of social justice, that is to say equality, in our society. For this reason I cannot accept the morality of large surtax reductions when the welfare services are attacked. I did not believe that Mr Heath could reduce prices 'at a stroke'. I saw his television interviews during the last days of the election campaign. He looked a desperate man clutching at any catchword which might bring him to power. Since the General Election we have seen the hollowness of the Conservative pledges.

Inflation has not been tackled. It is worse than ever before. A prices and incomes policy has been rejected; the Prices and Incomes Board was foolishly abolished. Hopes are placed on the Industrial Relations legislation which I regard as irrelevant, and the creation of a million unemployed which I regard as immoral. Since the Conservative Party is most readily brought to its senses through military parlance, I must state that my reaction to its economic and industrial measures is that you do not increase the emoluments of the officers when you are threatening to court-martial the other ranks.

I hope to return to Parliament as a Labour Member. I do not underrate the difficulties. Nor will my heart be broken if I should fail. I have sat on the back benches for seven years and I know the limitations of an MP's life. I am able to make my views known and thus possibly to influence public opinion because, almost without exception, newspaper editors and television producers have been consistently kind to me.

I do not suffer from the delusion that my absence from Parliament is widely regretted. I have ceased to be irritated by former parliamentary colleagues who greet me with the fatuous but well-intentioned question, 'When are you coming back to join us?' They speak as though I had wilfully mislaid a return railway ticket.

I remember in 1955 in the Carlton Club joining a recently retired Conservative MP at his solitary table. 'They miss me in the House,' he announced. Sensing a reaction on my part of mild but not, I hope, discourteous scepticism he launched into that declamation, stopping just short of a public address, which characterizes many elderly politicians. 'They all say to me "what we miss, Arthur, is your thorough good down-to-earth common sense". Mind you', and his voice dropped to a conspiratorial whisper, 'members of the Cabinet talk to me much more confidentially now that I am an elder statesman.' It was obviously grossly untrue. I found it pathetic but rather touching. Within two years he was dead.

The only former Conservative Member of Parliament, to my knowledge, to have been returned to Parliament at an election later, as a Labour supporter is Sir Oswald Mosley. Should I achieve this distinction, I shall hope to improve upon his subsequent performance.

Appendix I

Correspondence between Humphry Berkeley and Sir Alec Douglas-Home

1 January 1964

Dear Prime Minister,

In March of last year, before the leadership of the Party was in dispute, I said in public that I felt that the Conservative Party should adopt a more formal method of choosing a Leader. The events of the Blackpool Conference and after have, in my view, emphasized this need and would have done so, whoever had emerged as Leader of the Party.

Since then, I have had many talks with our colleagues in the House, including senior members of the Government. I have discovered a widespread view that we should not continue with the present system, which, in any event, as practised a few months ago, bore little resemblance to what has been known as the customary process.

The fact that the Chief Whip felt obliged to reveal in public a part but not all of the results of his soundings is evidence of the misgivings which are felt about the present process throughout the Party.

No doubt there are different views as to what formalized system should be adopted. Some would advocate a secret ballot of Members of Parliament voting for openly competing candidates. Others might extend the electoral college by including representatives of the candidates, the National Union and Peers in receipt of the Party whip. All these possibilities might be explored.

Would you consider, as Leader of the Party, setting up a small committee to consider this matter, hear opinions and make recommendations? I am sure that the whole issue could be considered more calmly at a time when there is no likelihood of it having to be implemented for some considerable period.

Nothing which I have said, of course, implies any criticism of your leadership of the Party.

May I take this opportunity of sending you every good wish for an outstandingly successful year.

Yours,

HUMPHRY BERKELEY

14 January 1964

My dear Berkeley,

Thank you for your letter of January 1.

I am not averse to the idea of a private study of the methods which might be used on some future occasion, but I do not think that it would be wise to initiate this before the Election.

It would inevitably become known, and would then be taken as evidence of dissatisfaction with the present leadership—although I appreciate your assurance that it does not.

If you will get in touch with me again later in the year, I will certainly consider what should then be done.

Yours ever,

ALEC DOUGLAS-HOME

21 January 1964

Dear Prime Minister,

Thank you for your letter of the 14th January. I am glad that you are prepared to consider the setting up of a private study to review the methods by which the Party Leader should be chosen.

I have passed the gist of your letter to some of my friends who have been interested in this problem. We are all happy to leave the matter in abeyance until after the Election, as you suggest. At the same time, I have made it clear to them that your decision has nothing to do with the Churchill/Macleod war, although this public wrangle could not have occurred if the secret ballot had been adopted.

I will write to you with detailed suggestions after the Election, but I think it is important to stress now that the study should not be so private as to prevent all interested parties from giving their views quite freely?

Yours,

HUMPHRY BERKELEY

6 November 1964

Dear Alec,

I was very glad that you said at the meeting of the 1922 Committee last night that you proposed to hold a review of the mechanism whereby the Leader of the Party is chosen. You will remember that we had an exchange of letters on this subject in January this year. You then said you were not averse to the idea of a private study of the methods which might be used on some future occasion, and you invited me to get in touch with you again after the Election. I have not done so until now, because I felt you must have had many other matters on your mind.

I should be very grateful if you could let me know in due course what form this assessment of the Party's views will take. I imagine you will appoint a committee before which one will be able to give evidence and views quite freely and in detail. It will, of course, be necessary that this committee should have the confidence of all sections of the Party, particularly in Parliament. I hope therefore, that the younger members of the Party will be adequately represented, since this would be in keeping with your own view of our need to look to the future and not to the past. I also hope that the evidence submitted to the committee and the conclusions arrived at by the committee will be made available in full to our colleagues in Parliament.

I would very much like to have a talk with you about these proposals when you can find time to see me.

Yours,

HUMPHRY

12th November 1964

My dear Humphry,

Thank you for your letter of the 6th November.

I am having some talks with Blakenham and others on the machinery for choosing a leader, and will get in touch when our ideas are a little further forward.

Yours ever,

ALEC

2 December 1964

My dear Alec,

You wrote to me on November 12 in reply to a letter of mine, when you said you would get in touch with me when you had discussed with John Blakenham the means whereby the Party's views on the selection of a new Leader might be ascertained.

Time is passing by, and I wonder whether you have yet decided whether you will appoint a small committee to go into this, or whether Blakenham alone will make an assessment. As I think you know, I strongly favour the former.

If, however, Blakenham is to make an assessment alone, ought not there to be some announcement about this, so that all interested parties know that he is now taking evidence? I would like to submit a memorandum to whatever body is considering the matter, but obviously cannot do so until the position is clarified in this respect.

Yours ever,
HUMPHRY

3 December 1964

My dear Humphry,

Many thanks for your letter of 2nd December.

I am so far handling this with a few colleagues to select and clarify the possibilities.

I should like to see any memorandum you have at this stage if I may.

Yours ever,
ALEC

9 December 1964

My dear Alec,

Many thanks for your letter of December 3, and for letting me know that you and a few colleagues are handling the matter at the present time.

I do hope that you will seriously consider the advantages

of making some sort of announcement of an official nature about this. It would be a very great pity if people with views on the matter were not to submit them through ignorance of how to do so, and, of course, there are obvious dangers in apparently dealing with this matter in a clandestine way.

I enclose a memorandum which states my own views, which I would be very glad to discuss with you or Blakenham if you would like me to do so.

Yours ever,
HUMPHRY

10 December 1964

My dear Humphry,
Thank you very much for the memorandum on *Choosing a Leader* which you sent with your letter of the 9th December.

Will you waylay me one day in the lobby, or look into my room?

Yours ever,
ALEC

15 December 1964

My dear Alec,
I was very glad to have an opportunity of talking to you yesterday afternoon, and I am delighted that you accept the three basic principles of procedure outlined in my memorandum—namely that Members of Parliament alone should vote, that they should do so by secret ballot, and that the result should be published. The more one thinks about the problem, the more one is driven to these conclusions.

Of course there still remains, as you said, the problem of what to do with the other members of the so-called Electoral College—the Peers, the prospective candidates and the members of the Executive of the National Union. You said that you thought they might be consulted before the vote took place, but it is very difficult to see what practical value this consultation would have if it is to be followed by a secret ballot to which none of them is party.

You also said that you thought it might be possible for them to nominate a candidate for Party Leader. There seems to be no reason why they should not do this, although it seems somewhat unlikely that anyone nominated by them would not in any event be nominated by Members of Parliament. What, of course, would be most undesirable, would be for an outside body of this character to have the power of vetoing a nomination before a vote of the Parliamentary Party were taken, but I understand that this is not in your mind at all.

On the whole I think there is much to be said for retaining the formal meeting of the Peers, Members of Parliament, prospective candidates and National Union Executive, at which the Party Leader has hitherto, as it were, been unveiled. Very few of those who have attended these meetings in the past have, until 1963, played any part at all in the choice of the Leader, but they have given formal endorsement to him in his capacity of Leader of the Party as a whole.

If this formal meeting is retained the Party is then able to make what is in practical terms a pretty drastic change, while preserving the outward appearance of continuity. In fact, in future, one man would be produced at the Party meeting who had been elected by secret ballot instead of one man who had been evolved in some other way.

It is a thousand pities that the National Union and the candidates were given a taste of apparent power in 1963, but there we are.

If this procedure were adopted it would be quite simple for you to say to our colleagues in Parliament that it was thought best that the Parliamentary Leader should be elected by a secret ballot of Members of Parliament. At the same time, you could let the Peers, the candidates and the National Union know that the Party meeting for endorsing the Leader would continue as in the past. The Peers, of course, could be given the right of electing the Leader of the Party in the House of Lords.

Yours ever,
HUMPHRY

15 December 1964

My dear Humphry,

Thank you very much for your letter of 15th December about our conversation yesterday on the machinery for selecting a Leader.

There is just one point in your first paragraph that I should like to clarify. I think it would be right that selection should be by secret ballot, and also that the result should be published, but with regard to the actual method of balloting, I would rather accept in principle that members of the House of Commons shall be in a dominating position in any ballot that is taken. It may well be that the final result of our thought on this will be that members of the House of Commons alone shall vote, but at this stage I would not like you to go away with the impression that this is my absolutely firm and final view, or that any other possible variation is entirely ruled out.

I shall continue my consultations and am sure that a satisfactory solution will be found.

Yours ever,
ALEC

28 December 1964

My dear Alec,

Thank you very much for your letter of December 15. I have delayed replying to you because I wished to think very carefully about your second paragraph, in which you said that with regard to the actual method of balloting you would rather accept in principle that Members of Parliament should be in a dominating position in any ballot which is taken. This would mean reverting to the idea of an Electoral College (which I had hoped had been thrown out of the window) in which presumably Peers, prospective candidates and the National Union would be represented.

I foresee very great difficulty in securing general agreement on the composition of such a College. Plainly the present

Party meeting would not be an acceptable body to the Members of Parliament, who are heavily outnumbered by others.

Can we be sure that the National Union, the Peers and the prospective candidates, once their right to participate in a vote had been conceded, would be willing to accept a defined proportion of votes in a new College which allowed the votes of Members of Parliament to predominate? Would, for example, the back-bench Peers be content to allow only the front-bench Peers to vote? How is any distinction to be made between one prospective candidate and another if they are not all to be included, and where does one draw the line with the National Union representatives? The entire National Union Executive Committee is too big since, in the circumstances of a severe defeat, this body could be as large as the Parliamentary Party. What body would have to approve this new arrangement? Would it be the Central Council or the Party conference? If the latter, how could one prevent things from getting completely out of control? Would the quota of votes given to each section of the Party be fixed for ever, or could this be overthrown at the whim of the Party conference?

I see no case for including prospective candidates in any ballot. The granting of the right to vote to members of the National Union, who are responsible to nobody, in the election of a Parliamentary Leader would be a step of great constitutional dubiety. It is sometimes argued that National Union representatives would ensure that the voice of the constituency associations was heard. I do not believe that on any sensible assessment it can be claimed that these people are more genuinely representative of Conservative Associations than their own Members of Parliament, who have been freely chosen and have been victorious at the polls. Peers are, of course, a part of Parliament, but I do not think it would be very wise to give a major voice in the choice of Parliamentary Leader to a non-elected body.

It is for these reasons that after much thought I have come to the conclusion that the actual ballot must be restricted to Members of Parliament alone. Nobody can in logic deny

Members of Parliament the right to elect their own Parliamentary Leader. The fact that the Parliamentary Leader is also in practice the Leader of the Party is a reflection of the importance which Parliament ought to occupy in our national political life.

The Party meeting should, in my view, be retained, without alteration. This body would meet to endorse as Leader of the Party someone who had already been elected by secret ballot as Leader of the Parliamentary Party. In theory, this endorsement could be refused. In practice, therefore, Members of Parliament would be most unlikely to choose someone who would not be acceptable to the Party as a whole. But a veto would exist.

Under this arrangement, historical continuity would be preserved, a balloting procedure would have been adopted which was manifestly above board, and it would not be necessary to secure the agreement of the Party conference or the Central Council to this change.

Yours ever,
HUMPHRY

31 December 1964

My dear Humphry,
Many thanks for your letter of the 28th December.

A plain House of Commons vote is one method and House of Commons domination another. The first is the simplest and simplicity has a lot to be said for it.

I very largely agreed with your broadcast. There is the Party meeting which already exists to confirm the choice of the House of Commons. This may suffice for the rest.

See me some time when we resume. I think in fact we are agreed.

Yours ever,
ALEC

Appendix II

The Berkeley Memorandum

1. In theory, different procedures for the choice of Leader have been applied depending on whether the Party is in power and its Leader is Prime Minister, or whether it is in opposition or, as in 1921, though part of the Government, its Leader was not Prime Minister.

2. Thus, in 1911 and 1921, Bonar Law and Austen Chamberlain were confirmed as Leaders of the Party in the House of Commons. (There was a Leader of the Party in the House of Lords who, in theory, had equal status). In 1902, 1922, 1923, 1937, 1940, 1955, 1957 and 1963, Balfour, Bonar Law, Baldwin, Neville Chamberlain, Churchill, Eden, Macmillan and Home were confirmed as Leaders of the Party as a whole. All were already Prime Minister with the exception of Bonar Law, who became so within a few hours of becoming Party Leader in October 1922.

3. In 1911 and 1921, the Leader of the Party in the House of Commons was formally endorsed in his position at meetings of the Conservative Members of Parliament. However, the Electoral College, which has always endorsed the leadership, has changed several times in this century. In 1902 and 1923 it consisted, in addition to Members of Parliament, of Peers in possession of the whip; in 1922, adopted prospective candidates were included. In 1937, 1940, 1955, 1957 and 1963, it consisted of Members of Parliament, Peers, adopted prospective candidates and members of the Executive Committee of the National Union.

4. It is not at all clear on whose authority prospective

candidates or members of the National Union Executive Committee were included in the Electoral College. However, since this College has never in fact voted, more attention may have been paid to filling a hall rather than devising a synod.

5. It is doubtful whether, in future, the Conservative Party could make a distinction between the position of Leader of the Party and that of Leader of the Party in the House of Commons. Today, whether the Party is in Government or Opposition, or whether the Party Leader in the Commons is Prime Minister or not, he is in fact the Leader of the Party as a whole.

6. In the past until 1963, despite differences in terminology as to the Leadership and differences in the composition of the Electoral College, the same procedures so far as the Party is concerned have in practice been applied. Soundings of influential people have been taken, a contest has been avoided, and when the Party has been in power, a Prime Minister has already been appointed. The Leader was then presented, amid universal acclaim, to the Electoral College, most of whom, until 1963, had not been consulted.

7. In 1963 it was recognized that there should be broader consultation than amongst members of the Cabinet or Members of Parliament. No doubt the announcement of Mr Macmillan's resignation to the Party Conference made this inevitable. Uncertainty as to who was entitled to be consulted, the absence of any formalized procedure, the fact that those who took soundings both decided who were to be sounded and what weighting was to be given to the opinions of those who had been sounded, and – most important of all – the fact that those who took the soundings and made the weightings were the only people to scrutinize the results of this somewhat arbitrary poll, has led to a feeling that this can never happen again.

8. If we are to adopt a formal process there should be three

basic principles of procedure: Members of Parliament alone should vote, they should do so by secret ballot, and the result should be published.

9. The Election should be confined to Members of Parliament, since it is on their support that the Leader is dependent in the House of Commons. There are no constitutional arguments in favour of the present so-called Electoral College, in which Members of Parliament are heavily outnumbered by Peers, prospective candidates (who have had no parliamentary experience) and members of the Executive Committee of the National Union—a body 150 strong, some of whom, although they do admirable voluntary work, represent nobody but themselves.

10. Any attempt to make Members of Parliament a minority voice in the Election of their Parliamentary Leader would still further erode the influence of Parliament as an institution. It would be most reprehensible for the Conservative Party to condone such a development.

11. A secret ballot is necessary so that Members of Parliament can quite freely express a preference without being subjected to any pressure or guidance from any quarter. The system of the alternative vote is desirable since this avoids the need for a second or third ballot some weeks later, as happens with the Labour Party, with the obvious dangers of delay and intrigue.

12. A published result is desirable because this is final and decisive. The day that Harold Wilson's victory over George Brown was announced, together with the voting figures, the personality squabbles in the Labour Party ceased. Had the Conservative Chief Whip been able to produce figures to support his statement that the wish of the majority of the Party had been followed in October 1963, the result could not have been queried from any quarter.

13. It should be possible for the Party to devise rules which

can be equally applicable to a situation of power or one of opposition. A Conservative Prime Minister should, in my view, resign first as Party Leader, thus enabling the Party to choose his successor. The Queen would then be spared the necessity of becoming involuntarily concerned in the internal politics of the Conservative Party by having to choose between rival Conservative leaders.

14. It is sometimes supposed that the choice by a political party, when in power, of a Parliamentary Leader who would automatically become Prime Minister represents an attack on the royal prerogative. This is not the case. Nor is the fact that a party which emerges victorious from a General Election already has a leader an attack on royal prerogative. The Queen had no alternative but to send for Mr Wilson in 1964, and the King had no alternative but to send for Mr Churchill in 1951. The prerogative is essentially concerned with situations such as arose in wartime in 1916 and 1940 and in a national emergency in 1931. The royal prerogative could conceivably have been involved had the result of the General Election been wholly indecisive. It is not part of the royal prerogative to do for the Conservative Party what it ought to be able to do for itself.

15. Provision should also be made for the periodical re-election of a Party Leader. It would probably be convenient for the Leader of the Party to be re-elected at the beginning of each Parliament.

Procedure for the Selection of the Leader of the Conservative and Unionist Party—announced by Sir Alec Douglas-Home in February 1965

1. There shall be a ballot of the Party in the House of Commons.

2. The Chairman of the 1922 Committee will be responsible for the conduct of the ballot and will settle all matters in relation thereto.

Nominations and Preparation of the Ballot

3. Candidates will be proposed and seconded in writing. The Chairman of the 1922 Committee and a body of scrutineers designated by him will be available to receive nominations. Each candidate will indicate on the nomination paper that he is prepared to accept nomination, and no candidate will accept more than one nomination. The names of the proposer and seconder will not be published and will remain confidential to the scrutineers. Nominations will close twenty-four hours before the first and second ballots. Valid nominations will be published.

4. The scrutineers will prepare a ballot paper listing the names of the candidates, and give a copy to each voter at a meeting called by the Chairman of the 1922 Committee for the pupose of balloting and consisting of all Members of the House of Commons in receipt of the Conservative and National Liberal Whips.

First Ballot

5. For the first ballot each voter will indicate one choice from the candidates listed, and hand the ballot paper to the scrutineers who will count the votes.

6. If as a result of this ballot one candidate both (i) receives an overall majority and (ii) receives 15 per cent more of the votes cast than any other candidate, he will be elected.

7. Scrutineers will announce the number of votes received by each candidate, and if no candidate satisfies these conditions, a second ballot will be held.

Second Ballot

8. The second ballot will be held not less than two days and not more than four days after the first ballot, excluding Saturdays and Sundays. Nominations made for the first

ballot will be void and new nominations, under the same procedure as for the first ballot, will be submitted for the original candidates if required and for any other candidate.

9. The voting procedure for the second ballot will be the same as for the first, save that paragraph 6 above shall not apply. If as a result of this second ballot one candidate receives an overall majority he will be elected.

Third Ballot

10. If no candidate receives an overall majority, the three candidates receiving the highest number of votes at the second ballot will be placed on a ballot paper for a third and and final ballot.

11. For the final ballot each voter must indicate two preferences amongst the three candidates by placing the figure '1' opposite the name of his preferred candidate and the figure '2' opposite the name of his second choice.

12. The scrutineers will proceed to add the number of first preference votes received by each candidate, eliminate the candidate with the lowest number of first preference votes and redistribute the votes of those giving him as their first preference amongst the two remaining candidates in accordance with their second preference. The result of this final count will be an overall majority for one candidate, and he will be elected.

Party Meeting

13. The candidate thus elected by the Commons Party will be presented for election as Party Leader to the Party Meeting constituted as at present.

Appendix III

Letter from Humphry Berkeley to Harold Wilson, dated 27 July 1970.

Dear Harold,

As you know I voted for the Labour Party in the recent General Election. I would like to apply for the membership of the Party.

I am deeply disturbed at the Conservative attitude over the sale of arms to South Africa, in opposition to the vote of the United Nations Security Council. It is far from clear even now that this sale will not take place. I am also fundamentally opposed to further talks with the Smith regime to which the Conservatives are committed which seem to me to be quite pointless after an election has been held in Rhodesia on the new illegal constitution. I was deeply dismayed at the Conservative Party's support for the South African Cricket Tour; and I have come to the conclusion that its leaders are wholly unaware of the great dangers which lie ahead in Southern Africa, which may end in racial violence there which would have far wider repercussions elsewhere.

May I also say how much I deplore the personal attacks which have been made on your personal integrity by Conservatives including members of the present Government during the past five years. It has seemed to be not only respectable, but almost obligatory for them to refer to you in terms that I would hesitate to use about a convicted criminal. I am not prepared to participate in politics on this level. I believe that as Prime Minister you showed outstanding flair and courage. Whilst of course nobody would suggest that mistakes were not made during the past five and a half years, your great achievement has been to transform the Labour Movement from a party of protest into a party of power.

I would like to help the Labour Party, in whatever way I can, to return to power at the next General Election.

Of all the expressions in the English language, perhaps the most unpleasant is that of turncoat. I have no doubt that this will be levelled at me. I can however claim some consistency in my views since I spoke in favour of a total arms embargo against South Africa in the House of Commons as long ago as 1963. I thought and said that even the *Tiger* and *Fearless* proposals for Rhodesia went further than I was prepared to go to accommodate Ian Smith.

I left the Conservative Party at a point when it was at the height of popularity, not only in the now discredited polls, but also in terms of by-election results. I am joining the Labour Party on the morrow of its defeat. I cannot promise to be entirely docile, but I will be indefatigable.

With kind regards,
Yours sincerely,
HUMPHRY BERKELEY

Mr Wilson's reply to Humphry Berkeley dated 28 July 1970

Dear Humphry,
Thank you for your letter of 27 July which, of course, I was very glad to receive.

I greatly welcome your decision to join the Labour Party and your statement of your reasons for doing so.

I was glad, too, to hear you explain these in greater detail on *The World at One* today.

As you will know, membership of the Labour Party is not a matter for decision by the Leader of the Party, but I understand you are already in touch with the General Secretary. As you know, the next step will be for you to join your own Constituency Party. I am sure they will be very pleased indeed to receive your application.

Yours,
HAROLD WILSON

Index